Health and the Construction of the Individual

D0226298

How do social scientists create facts? What strategies do they use to construct knowledge? How does social science make sense of the individual? Critical studies of both medical and scientific knowledge have been conducted but social science knowledge remains relatively unquestioned.

Addressing this question, *Health and the Construction of the Individual* is a social study of social science. Jane Ogden focuses particularly on constructions of the individual in health-related psychology and sociology. She explores how social science texts construct social science facts using the strategies of theory, methodology, measurement and rhetorical boundaries and argues that the individual is not only constructed through the dissemination of social science knowledge but through the mechanics of its production. The results provide a unique insight into the transformation of the individual as an ever-changing self, from both a historical and social constructionist perspective.

Health and the Construction of the Individual will make fascinating reading for health psychologists, medical sociologists, social constructionists and all students and researchers interested in gaining a greater understanding of the premises underlying social science.

Jane Ogden completed her PhD at the Institute of Psychiatry and is now a Reader in Health Psychology at Guy's, King's and St Thomas' School of Medicine where she teaches medical and psychology students. Her previous publications include two books on diet, a textbook in Health Psychology and numerous papers in the health field.

Health and the Construction of the Individual

Jane Ogden

First published 2002 by Routledge
27 Church Road, Hove, East Sussex, BN3 2FA

Simultaneously published in the USA and Canada
by Taylor & Francis Inc,
29 West 35th Street, New York, NY 10001

Routledge is an imprint of the Taylor & Francis Group
http://www.tandf.co.uk

© 2002 Jane Ogden

Typeset in Times by Mayhew Typesetting, Rhayader, Powys
Printed and bound in Great Britain by Biddles Ltd, Guildford and
King's Lynn

British Library Cataloguing in Publication Data
A catalogue record for this book is available from the British Library

Library of Congress Cataloging-in-Publication Data
A catalog record for this book is available from the Library of
Congress

ISBN 0-415-23306-2 (hbk)
ISBN 0-415-23307-0 (pbk)

Contents

Illustrations

Acknowledgements

This book is the consequence of discussions with colleagues, presentations at conferences and papers which included some of the ideas in their preliminary stages. I am therefore grateful to all those who have helped either directly or indirectly with this book. In particular I would like to thank David Armstrong for his comments, suggestions and discussions, the referees for their constructive and sometimes critical comments which have moved the book along, and to Beryl Stevens for typing the references.

This book has developed out of a series of papers and presentations and I am grateful to the following for permission to publish extracts from these publications:

Taylor & Francis: Ogden, J. (1995) Changing the subject of Health Psychology. *Psychology and Health*, 10, 257–265.

Sage Publications: Ogden, J. (1997) The rhetoric and reality of psycho-social theories: a challenge to biomedicine? *Journal of Health Psychology*, 2, 21–29.

Lucy Yardley: Ogden, J. (1997) Diet as a vehicle for self control. In L. Yardley (ed), *Material Discourses of Health and Illness*, 199–216. London: Routledge.

Psychology Press: Ogden, J. (2001) Theory and Measurement: conceptualisation, operationalisation and the example of health status. In A. Vingerhoets (ed), *Assessment in Behavioral Medicine*. Hove: Brunner-Routledge.

1 Introduction

Towards a social study of social science

Overview

In 1968 James Watson published his personal account of the discovery of
the structure of DNA in which he described a meeting with Francis Crick
soon after they realised that DNA was in the form of a double helix:

> When the Eagle opened at six I went over with Francis to talk about
> what must be done in the next few days. Francis wanted no time lost in
> seeing whether a satisfactory three dimensional model could be built,
> since the geneticists and nucleic acid biochemists should not misuse
> their time and facilities any longer than necessary. They must be told
> the answer quickly, so that they could reorient their research upon our
> work . . . I thought more about Linus and the possibility that he might
> stumble upon the base pairs before we told him the answer.
>
> (Watson, 1968, p. 156)

There are three different ways of reading this excerpt. First, to a scientist it
provides some interesting background information to one of the most
important scientific discoveries of the twentieth century. It therefore adds
some human interest to a great scientific finding. Second, to an avid reader
of autobiographies it provides some interesting insights into the people
themselves. It reveals the impatient nature of Crick and the competitiveness
of Watson. In contrast, a third reading would fall into the camp of those
interested in the social studies of science. From this perspective this text
(referred to as 'discourse') provides information on how the facts about
DNA (referred to as the 'object' of this discourse) were produced. The first
two analyses from the worlds of science and autobiography form part of
conventional wisdom and are covered in depth within the fields of jour-
nalism, literature and history. The third analysis reflects a more unconventional approach and informs this book. In particular, this book aims to
examine not how scientific discourse produces scientific facts but how social
science discourse produces social science facts. To this end this introductory
chapter will first ask 'what is a discourse?' and 'what is an object?' It will

then explore the object of social science, the individual, with a focus on the many descriptions of the self. Second, this chapter will examine the ways in which a discourse and its object may interrelate and describe the emergence of social constructionism as the umbrella theoretical approach for this work. Third, this chapter will explore the social studies of science perspective and describe how it emerged out of social constructionism. Finally, the chapter will outline the aims and structure of this book and suggest that not only can there be a social studies of science but also a social studies of social science.

What is a discourse?

The term *discourse* appears in a range of areas of study and implies an increasing number of meanings. For example, in linguistics it is used to describe how propositions are linked together to form a linguistic unit larger than a sentence and in psycholinguistics it describes any utterance within the context of communication. In contrast, in literary theory, discourse signals a way of breaking up the divisions between literary and non-literary texts and within political and feminist works discourse describes ideological clusters such as 'patriarchal discourses' and 'capitalist discourses'. Within social science, however, discourse is mainly used to describe the verbal reports of individuals. In particular, discourse is analysed by those who are interested in language and talk and what people are doing with their speech. This has tended to be the domain of critical social psychologists. For example, such researchers examine the function of rhetorical devices (e.g. Billig *et al.*, 1988), how accounts of the social world are constructed and what impact these accounts have on the speaker (Potter and Wetherell, 1987). This perspective is often called 'discourse analysis' and is informed by approaches such as speech act theory, ethnomethodology and conversational analysis. In line with this, Potter and Edwards (1992) suggested that 'the focus of discursive psychology is the action orientation of talking and writing' (p. 2) and the study of what 'talk and writing is being used to do'. Harré and Gillett drew on Wittgenstein and argued that discourse plays a central part in what is termed the 'second cognitive revolution' as 'concepts, the basis of thinking are expressed by words and words are located in languages which are used to accomplish a huge variety of tasks' (Harré and Gillett, 1994, p. 21). Such discourse analysts study what individuals say and what they are achieving by saying it. In a similar vein research has also examined the nature of speech between people. This has focused either on the way in which the speaker and listener use tactics of evasion and refutation (Bloor and McIntosh, 1990) or in terms of the use of silences, omissions and hesitations (Chase, 1995). Therefore such researchers analyse discourse as a means to explore what is said by people either on their own or when interacting with others and conceptualise discourse in terms of what is said (or not said) by individuals. This approach to discourse often involves the collection of data using in-depth interviews or focus groups and can be understood as discourse at the micro level.

In contrast, the term *discourse* is also used to refer to meanings at the more macro level. This approach does not study the individual words spoken by people but the language used to describe aspects of the world, and has tended to be taken by those using a sociological perspective. For example, Sontag explored the discourses around illness and described how illnesses such as cancer and HIV are made sense of by those who write about them (Sontag, 1977). Likewise, Weeks explored sexual discourses (Weeks, 1985), Armstrong explored the discourses concerned with the body (Armstrong, 1983, 2002), Foucault explored the discourses concerned with punishment (Foucault, 1979), and Wetherell and Potter (1992) examined racist discourse. These approaches have not used talk as their discourse but written texts found in books, leaflets, advertisements and both academic and popular papers. Such texts are conceptualised as discourse and read in the same way that an interview transcript would be read for its meaning. If discourses are concerned with meanings then any text which can be 'read' can be considered a discourse; a much broader definition than that concerned with micro-level discourse. In fact, studies exploring discourse at the macro level have often expanded the definition of discourse further to include what Foucault has called 'discursive practices'. This definition of discourse focuses not only on talk and written texts but also on behaviour and action. For example, the use of a stethoscope, the prescribing of medicine, the process of surgery can be seen as medical discursive practices (Foucault, 1973). In addition, the interventions surrounding childbirth such as episiotomies, epidurals and caesarians can be seen as gendered discursive practices (e.g. Armstrong, 1983). From this perspective a discourse is any behaviour (including speech) which is embedded with representation and meaning.

This separation between micro- and macro-level discourses is an artificial one however, as many writers explore how individuals draw upon macro discourses in their speech and illustrate how macro discourses permeate and construct the micro-level discourses found in conversation. For example, Potter and Wetherell (1987) suggested that individuals in conversation with each other draw on shared 'interpretive repertoires' in order to explain or persuade. Similarly, Gill (1993) suggested that people call upon 'practical ideologies' when trying to either include or exclude each other. Billig *et al.* (1988) suggested that individuals weigh up contrasting public and collective views called 'ideological dilemmas' when attempting to position themselves within a social interaction. In addition, Burman and Parker (1993) argued that 'our talk and writing is constructed out of existing resources' and that 'these resources are the repertoires, repertoires we do not create ourselves anew when we speak but which we have to borrow and refashion for our own purposes' (p. 4). Macro discourses are seen to inform and even create the micro discourses.

Figure 1.1   What is discourse?

In summary, the term *discourse* can refer to talk or speech. It can also mean clusters of beliefs, written texts or behaviour and action. It also reflects how these micro and macro levels of discourse influence each other (see Figure 1.1). When discourse is explored it is often examined to see what it can reveal about its 'object'. This raises the question 'what is an object?'

What is an object?

The nature of an object (or thing, or identity) has been addressed extensively by philosophers and linguists such as Frege, Quine and Leibniz. From this perspective an object has been defined in terms of 'whatever may be referred to by a proper name', or the opposite of self or person. Although social scientists attempt to define discourse, they have neglected the question 'what is an object?' The answer to this question can be facilitated by drawing upon a wide range of social science literatures which, although they do not explicitly define their objects, illustrate implicit definitions. First, within psychology, psycholinguistics, for example, is concerned with language as a representation of the real world. Garnham (1985) argued that 'under-standing language requires the construction of or reference to internal mental representations of how things are or might be' (p. 3). He stated that 'language is about the world' (p. 15) and suggested that to understand this real world it is first necessary to decode the input and then to develop a mental model of the part of the world being represented. Psycholinguists therefore define their object via an exploration of two processes: word recognition (defining the input; what is it?) and word meaning (understand-ing the world being represented; what does it mean?). The first process of word recognition is described as involving the activation of a 'mental lexicon', the selection of a number of suitable words on the basis of perceptual and contextual information and the gradual rejection of the wrong words. Garnham described how 'word recognition is achieved when there is only one remaining candidate and the input has been identified' (p. 43). The second process of understanding word meaning follows a similar pattern. It is argued that once a word has been recognised its features are then assessed to determine what it means. This involves the activation of a semantic memory and a classification of the word according to what are called its 'truth conditions' involving 'set inclusion' (e.g. a dog has four legs) and 'antonymy' (e.g. it is not a cat). It also describes how each word has an associated 'distinguisher' to decide what the word is similar and dissimilar to. Therefore, the semantic memory is searched to find the meaning associated with the identified word by accepting words which are similar and rejecting words which are dissimilar. Psycholinguistics is the study of language and how it represents the outside world. The object within psycholinguistics is defined through a process of acceptance and rejection of alternatives.

In parallel, a similar definition of the object can be seen within the cognitive psychology literature and its exploration of object recognition. Sutherland (1973) suggested that seeing and identifying objects involves the activation of a 'stored description' of an object which is defined in terms of a range of 'structural descriptions'. For example, a dog may have a structural description of 'tail', and the letter 'T' may have the structural description of 'horizontal and vertical bar'. Therefore in parallel to the object of psycholinguistics, recognising the object studied by cognitive psychology involves activating all similar object descriptions and rejecting those which do not fit.

Social psychology also implicitly describes its object. Group identity provides an example (Brown, 1986). Research exploring group identity suggested that group membership is defined in terms of in-group and out-group identities. It is also argued that stereotypes and prejudices are maintained through attributions made about the out group and that ethnocentrism is fundamental to any group cohesiveness. The object of group identity is therefore defined both in terms of what is in the group and what has been left out. One object of developmental psychology, the self, is also defined implicitly. Central to developmental psychology is the concept of the 'self' as separate from 'the other'. For example, the process called 'object permanence' is centred on an exploration of how infants can differentiate between an object's existence when they can see it and its continuing existence even when they cannot (Piaget, 1954). This involves a differentiation between the self and the world. Similarly, developmental psychologists have examined the development of the theory of mind (Premack and Woodruff, 1978). This described how infants and children differentiate between their own mind and that of others, but are able to impute from their own experiences the possible experiences of others. Therefore, being able to say 'I cannot see something but I know you can' is illustrative of a theory of mind. Accordingly, the object of developmental psychology, the self, is defined by differentiating it from both 'the world' and 'the other'.

In short, psycholinguistics defines its objects (the words and their meanings) via a process of differentiation between similarity and dissimilarity. Cognitive psychologists define their object (an object) in terms of matching and non-matching, and social psychology defines its object (the group) in terms of membership and non-membership. Likewise, developmental psychology defines its object (the self) in terms of 'not the world' and 'not other'. These psychological literatures leave the definition of an object as implicit, yet they utilise the same underlying method of object definition. From these diverse literatures an object is consistently characterised by two dimensions: 'what it is' and 'what it is not'. This definition of an object can also be seen to permeate both sociology and social anthropology. For example, Durkheim (1915) argued that central to any analysis and definition of society was the differentiation between the sacred and profane. Incorporated into the definition of what was sacred was that it was not profane – sacred was defined in terms of what it was not. Drawing upon this perspective, Douglas (1966) examined the management and definition of pollution and the rituals apparent in 'primitive' societies. In particular, she focused on the boundaries between 'things' and suggested that 'it is only by exaggerating the difference between within and without, above and below, male and female, with and against, that semblance of order is created' (p. 4). Accordingly, she suggested that boundaries create order. She also discussed the dangers inherent at the point of the boundary and the problems with matter such as 'spittle, blood, milk, urine, faeces or tears' which she argues 'by simply tearing forth have traversed the boundary of the body' (p. 121). She described rituals such as carrying the bride over the threshold, and the concern with food cleanliness as ways of managing boundary issues. In addition, she used the concept of 'dirt' as 'essentially disorder' and states that 'dirt offends against order' (p. 2). Therefore, Douglas argued that concepts of purity and pollution highlight the importance of boundaries (both social and body) and that objects are defined both by what they are (on one side of the boundary) and what they are not (on the other side). This also finds reflection in the work of Popper who has relevance to a range of literatures (e.g. Popper, 1959). Popper argued that any fact should be examined within the processes of falsification and

Table 1.1   What is an object?

The object	What it is	What it is not
word	matching	difference
meaning	set inclusion	antonymy
object	accepting	rejecting
group	in group	out group
individual	self	other
society	sacred	profane
dirt	danger	purity
fact	verification	falsification

verification. Therefore, within these apparently disparate psychological, sociological and social anthropological literatures an object is consistently defined as what it is and what it is not (see Table 1.1). Further, although there are multiple facets of the social science object, this object consistently relates to aspects of the individual.

The object of social science: the individual

Social science is concerned with the study of the individual, and the characteristics of this individual have been explored and assessed in terms of descriptions of the self. For example, Stevens (1996a) examined the different ways in which the self has been studied within psychology and highlighted different theoretical perspectives, different methodological approaches and different underlying assumptions. Giddens (1991) also analysed the self from a sociological perspective, and writers such as Gergen (1991), Harré (1983), Baumeister (1986) and Cushman (1990) have offered their own analyses of the nature of the self at differing times in history. Some of these multiple selves will be considered here.

Social science has described a 'biological self' which has emphasised the role of physiology in the form of neurons, synapses and genetics (e.g. Toates, 1996). This type of individual is understood in terms of their evolutionary history and the impact of their physiological systems in determining behaviour and cognitions. The 'biological self' is central to sociobiology with its emphasis on genetic explanations of gender, class and ethnic differences and also forms the basis of evolutionary psychology. A 'biological self' has also emerged as part of discussions concerning the importance of embodiment and the embodied self (e.g. Giddens, 1991; Radley, 1993, 1997). For example, Giddens (1991) argued 'The self, of course, is embodied' (p. 56) and 'the reflexivity of the self extends to the body' (p. 77).

Social science has also described an 'interpreting self' (Lalljee, 1996). Such an individual is central to much experimental and observational work within psychology and is described in terms of the processes of categorisation and their capacity to process information. Research interested in the 'interpreting self' explores stereotypes, individuals' explanatory styles and feelings of control in terms of constructs such as learned helplessness, mastery and attributions. Central to this area of work are researchers such as Heider (1958) with his work on interpersonal relations and his study of how people make sense of the world, Jones (e.g. 1979) who studied the fundamental attribution error and the tendency to infer attitudes and personality from behaviour, and Seligman's work on learned helplessness and the hypothesised link with depression (Seligman, 1975).

Giddens (1991) also examined the nature of the self in the 'late modern age' and stated that the self could be considered self-aware and as illustrative of 'high reflexivity'; the 'reflexive self'. He stated that self-identity 'is the self as reflexively understood by the person in terms of her or his biography' (p. 53). He also argued that there was a 'reflexive shaping of identity' and that the self had become a 'reflexive project' which was created and sustained through biography, and an ever-changing narrative of self-identity. Accordingly, he indicated that the identity of the self is created and re-created and that 'we are not what we are, but what we make of ourselves', and that 'what the individual becomes is dependent on the reconstructive endeavours in which he or she engages' (p. 75). Stevens (1996c) also described the 'reflexive self' as central to research on experience and subjectivity which is studied drawing upon perspective such as phenomenology, humanistic psychology and existential psychology. Researchers who have studied the 'reflexive self' include Csikszentmihalyi (1992) who focused on consciousness and described 'entropy' as being when thoughts intrude upon consciousness, causing disorder and 'flow' when incoming information is congruent with goals. Similarly, Donaldson (1992) described the development of consciousness through a series of stages, and Kelly (1955, 1980) emphasised personal constructs as being the key dimensions which underlie an individual's experience of the world. Within such research the 'reflexive self' is described as having the experience that one is existing, being an active intentional agent and possessing reflexive awareness.

Social science has also described a 'social self' as being an individual who has merged within their social context whereby the person, their consciousness and their self are seen as social (Wetherell and Maybin, 1996). For example, Rosaldo (1984) described feelings as 'not substances to be discovered in our blood but social practices organised by stories that we both enact and tell'. This individual is the focus of 'sociological social psychology' and is often studied within the perspective of social constructionism (Wetherell and Maybin, 1996). The 'social self' is explored with an emphasis on discourse, discursive practices and the importance of talk. As Bruner (1986) argued, 'our sensitivity to narrative provides the major link between our own sense of self and sense of others in the social world around us' (p. 69).

Gergen has also studied the individual and described the 'saturated self' (1991). This self is considered to have been over-exposed to the 'technologies of social saturation' from social life, television, video, magazines, telephones, newspapers and junk mail. In particular, Gergen emphasised the impact of virtual social practices and interactions which remove us from 'real' engagement which is replaced by engagement at a distance and partial engagement. The 'saturated self' is considered 'too full' and to be a state of 'introjective overload' so that 'one begins to experience the vertigo of unlimited multiplicity' (1991, p. 49). In a contrasting model of the self, Cushman (1990) described the 'empty self'. He argued that 'the current self is constructed as empty' as the individual 'experiences a significant absence of community, tradition and shared meaning' (1990, p. 600). This self is seen as one which has lost a sense of self-worth and personal conviction, and is left with a gaping hunger which needs to be sated.

Bruner also described the 'distributed self'. Such an individual is the 'sum and swarm of participations in social life' (1990, p. 107). The identity of this individual is multifaceted and has many different contextually dependent selves which can be seen as 'continually spreading, changing, grouping and regrouping across a relational and social field' (Wetherell and Maybin, 1996, p. 222). The 'distributed self' is not a unitary self, as many other descriptions of the individual have implied, but an ever-changing and flexible self full of contradictions who responds to different contexts with different self-presentations.

From a different perspective, Thomas (1996) described the 'defensive self' to delineate the ways in which the self has been described using psycho-analysis as a methodology for studying subjective experience. It is argued that the 'defensive self' is an individual whose conscious awareness is just the tip of the iceberg of their experience and that a large portion of sub-jectivity is beyond consciousness and subjugated by the dynamic driving force of the unconscious. Accordingly, the 'defensive self' experiences and presents to the world a biased version of what is known and what has been experienced, as much experience cannot be accessed and remains hidden. From this perspective self-hood is inaccessible, the individual is therefore not fully reflexive and much of the self is repressed by societal taboos and rules of conduct. Researchers who have explored the 'defensive self' include Winnicott (1960) who argued that an individual's true self can be impinged upon by childhood experience and subsequently hidden in the unconscious, and that a conscious and compliant false self can be projected to the world as a form of self-protection. Other selves which have been explored include the 'private self' (Rose, 1985, 1990), the 'risky self' (Ogden, 1995a) and the 'minimalist self' (Lasch, 1984).

In sum, a discourse can therefore be defined as either micro or macro or a synthesis of the two. An object can be defined in terms of what it is and what it is not. For social science this object is consistently the individual who has been described in terms of a multitude of different selves. Social scientists have differing ways of understanding how discourse and its object relate to each other.

Discourse and its object

Linguists describe the relationship between language and its object in the real world, those studying semiotics explore the relationship between the signifier and the signified, cognitive psychologists examine the relationship between mental representations and that which is being represented, and social scientists increasingly analyse the relationship between a discourse and its object (Table 1.2). All these dichotomies are characterised by the issue of representation and the 'aboutness' of the relationship. Language is about the real world, the signifier is about the signified, a mental represen-tation is about the object being represented and discourse is about its

Table 1.2   *Representation*

Representation ... (about) ...	*Object*
noun	thing
'table'	table
landscape picture	landscape
portrait picture	person
photography	world
image	reality
memory	event
signifier	signified
discourse	object

object. However, the nature of this 'aboutness' is not always the same – each dichotomy has been explored from several different perspectives. This is particularly the case for the relationship between discourse and its object. The range of differing perspectives can be categorised into three main models shown in Figure 1.2.

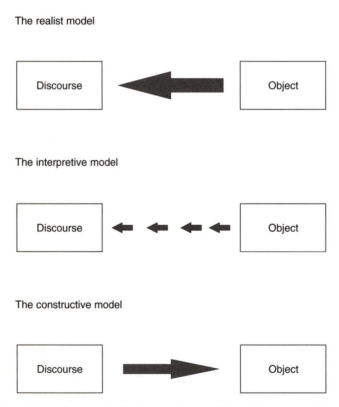

Figure 1.2   The realist model, the interpretive model and the constructive model

A realist model

According to a realist model, the relationship between discourse and its object is unproblematic; discourses simply describe their world. This perspective is in line with the scientific tradition and incorporates the perspectives of empiricism and positivism. For example, discourses which describe sex as biological can be seen to reflect the truth about sex – if sex is described as biological then it is biological. Likewise, those which report the results from their scientific studies are understood as unproblematic depictions of facts – the data and the reports of those data simply describe what was really found. Using the realist model a discourse describes and reflects its object.

An interpretive model

An alternative approach to discourse and its object suggests a more complex relationship: a theoretical approach which highlights an interpretive relationship suggests that discourse does not simply describe its object but makes sense of and interprets it. Therefore, discourses which describe sex as biological would be understood as one possible way of making sense of the world. Likewise, the results from research study would be considered an interpretation of the data. Accordingly, from an interpretive perspective discourses are an interpretation, rather than a pure reflection of their object.

The constructive model

A third and increasingly subscribed to model of the discourse/object relationship suggests that discourses may not simply describe the world, or even interpret the world. An approach which emphasises a problematic relationship suggests that discourses construct their world. Within this framework, the role of the world becomes minimised and discourses are conceptualised as all-important. For example, a discourse which describes sex as biological is considered to actually construct sex as being biological. Likewise, results from a research study which illustrate gender differences are understood as actually creating these differences. Therefore, from this perspective discourse constructs its object.

These three analyses illustrate differing ways of conceptualising the relationship between discourse and its object and indicate a transition from prioritising the reality and truth of the object over the discourse (the realist model), to emphasising the transformation of the object by discourse (the interpretive model), to prioritising the discourse (the constructive model). The emergence of social constructionism reflects an interest in an increasingly problematic relationship between discourse and its object and a shift away from a realist model towards one which emphasises the discourse as constructive.

The emergence of social constructionism

The scientific tradition up until the 1960s focused on the development of ever-improved ways to access the truth about the world. For scientists interested in biochemistry or physics, some of this involved laboratory research; for those involved in the anatomy of the body, dissection may have provided the way forward; and for those interested in the individual, surveys, experiments and face-to-face interviews were the chosen methods. Science was a fact-finding exercise and social science followed in its footsteps. From this perspective, which has often been called a realist one, the knowledge and facts produced by research were seen as unproblematic, and the rejection of old truths and the acceptance of new ones was seen as a welcome indication of progress. From the 1960s however, there have been several challenges to this position. From psychology and psychiatry came the anti-psychiatry movement pioneered by Szasz (1961) who argued that whereas physical illnesses were real, mental illness was a product of labelling, social norms and the psychiatric drive for social control. This was supported by the works of Goffman (1961) and Rosenhan (1973) who described the functioning of 'asylums' and their methods for creating psychiatric problems. Such writers therefore problematised psychiatric facts. From a broader perspective came the works of Berger and Luckman (1967) who challenged the notion of everyday facts and argued that individuals both construct their world and experience the world as pre-constructed. Writers also problematised the notion of scientific facts. For example, Kuhn (1962) argued that scientific truths and the disciplines which produce and study them are products of social processes inherent within the social communities themselves. This analysis was developed by Young in his paper 'Science is social relations' (1977). In addition, writers have also turned to medical facts and the nature of the body and argued that not only is psychiatric illness a social product but physical illness and the associated physical bodily structures are as well. For example, studies have examined changes over time for the experience of illness (Duden, 1991), notions of sexuality, the nature of the clinic, the nature of punishment (Foucault, 1973, 1979, 1981), descriptions of mortality, the structure of the hospital and rules of hygiene (Armstrong, 1986, 1993, 1998). These authors have suggested that changes in the way in which these aspects of the physical world are depicted are not reflections of an improved understanding of the truth but illustrate how the truths themselves have changed across time. Therefore since the 1960s the nature of 'the fact' has been challenged. Such challenges fall under the broad umbrella of social constructionism which suggests that truth and fact are problematic concepts and are constructed out of social processes, social relations and social interactions. Although there are several different versions of social constructionism ranging from the weak to the strong programme which vary in their conceptualisation of the relationship between discourse and its object, in general, social constructionism tends towards a more problematic view of the discourse/ object relationship. In line with this, Szasz challenged the assumed relationship between the diagnosis of mental illness and the reality of an illness. Likewise, Foucault explored the relationship between descriptions of the body and the body as it is and Kuhn problematised the relationship between scientific facts and the world outside being studied. In the footsteps of Kuhn, the social studies of science turned its attention to the scientific fact.

The social studies of science

Up until about 1960, science was seen as a straightforward investigation of the world. Biochemists studied chemical reactions, physicists studied matter and energy, ethologists studied animal behaviour and biologists studied the physiology and anatomy of animals and plants. Scientists carried out their work in a straightforward and unproblematic way. In the 1970s however, science itself became the focus of study. The social studies of science was developed as a subdiscipline of social science, particularly sociology, and turned its attention to the study of science and the scientists themselves. In particular, the social studies of science was grounded in an interest in the scientific production of knowledge. For example, Bloor, one of its key figures, opened his book *Knowledge and Social Imagery* (1976) with the question, 'Can the sociology of knowledge investigate and explain the very content and nature of scientific knowledge?'' (p. 1). He therefore argued that the sociological imagination should and could be turned to an evaluation of science and the scientific method. In the light of this proposal, writers such as Woolgar (e.g. Lynch and Woolgar, 1988; Woolgar, 1981, 1988), Mulkay (1991) and Latour (Latour, 1987; Latour and Woolgar, 1986) have studied science and scientists with an emphasis on how science produces scientific facts.

This approach has involved detailed examinations of the range of methods used by scientists. In particular, those working within the social studies of science have explored the networks of communication and social relationships between scientists. They have carried out a study of laboratory culture and the mechanics of laboratory research, and have examined the role of company managers and the influence of the scientific community. In addition, they have analysed the functioning of a physics department, the development of machinery and have assessed the research stations of radio astronomy. The day-to-day lives of scientists have come under 'scientific scrutiny'. This work has produced detailed accounts of 'science in action' and has classified and categorised the processes which are involved in the production of scientific facts. For example, it has described factors such as 'actor networks' to illustrate how scientists recruit their colleagues for support and states that these networks are essential for building individual careers and turning one finding by one scientist into an accepted truth. The writers have also coined the term 'a black box' to represent evidence which has become an accepted fact and therefore remains unchallenged, and have argued that once a finding has been 'black boxed' it requires much effort on behalf of dissenting researchers to unbox it. In addition, those involved in this field have written about 'action at a distance' to illustrate how one scientist's theories can be promoted by others working in other laboratories or even other countries.

Using this perspective science can therefore be analysed in the same way that scientists themselves analyse their own data. The social studies of science examines science and the production of the scientific fact, and views science as a discourse and the scientific fact as the object of this discourse. It has taken a social constructionist view of the relationship between discourse and its object and has argued that rather than simply describing its object, or even interpreting it, discourse actually constructs its object. From this perspective scientific facts are constructed, not revealed by their 'discovery'.

The social studies of science, therefore, analyses science and explores the role of scientific discourse in the production of the scientific fact. To this end, it locates scientific discourse and its object within a given space and time. It also analyses the ways in which scientific discourse produces the object of science. To do so it draws upon social science literature – particularly social constructionism. But what about social science discourse and the social scientific fact? Can these also be located within a given space and time? And can the impact of social science discourse on the object of social science also be examined? Some writers have also turned their analysis on to social science itself.

When describing the object of social science (the individual), much research has highlighted a range of possible selves using different methodologies and different theoretical perspectives. In the main, this approach has considered the different selves to co-exist and to be independent of their history or the culture within which they have been described. Some writers, however, have located contemporary descriptions of the self within a given space and time. For example, Giddens (1991) placed his 'reflexive self' firmly in the late modern era and argued that this self is a product of this age. Gergen (1991) located his 'saturated self' in the conditions of a modern society and Cushman (1990) situated his 'empty self' at the end of the twentieth century. Likewise, Bruner (1990) argued that the 'distributed self' was a product of its time, and Thomas (1996) suggested that the 'defensive self' as described within psychoanalysis has changed over time and has become 'more fluid and constructed' (p. 324).

Some writers have also explored the ways in which this object of social science has been produced by the social science discourse. The main thrust of Giddens' argument (1991) is an examination of the institutions of modernity and the ways in which these institutions construct the self as reflexive and contribute towards the reflexive project. He also, however, analysed the literature from social research and argued that 'sociology and the social sciences more widely conceived are inherent elements of the institutional reflexivity of modernity' and that social research 'are not just works about social processes, but the materials which in some part constitute them' (p. 2). In particular, Giddens (1991) drew upon studies such as 'Second chances' by Wallerstein and Blakeslee (1989), *Studies in Ethnomethodology* by Garfinkel (1984) and *Self Therapy* by Rainwater (1989), and examined how these studies contributed towards the reflexive project and self-identity.

The relationship between social science discourse and its object has also been studied more explicitly by Rose (1985, 1990). He provided a detailed analysis of the impact of psychological knowledge on the changing nature of subjectivity and illustrated the complex relationship between 'technologies of subjectivity' and subjectivity. Specifically, Rose explored the institutions and organisations which draw upon psychological expertise such as the military, therapists, schools, counsellors and businesses, and argued that by using and being informed by psychological knowledge, such centres of power shape the way in which we think about ourselves. Therefore, Rose explored the discourse of psychology found within these 'new forms of power' and assessed their influence on 'the private self'. In a similar vein, the collaborative text *Changing the Subject* (Henriques *et al.*, 1984) also examined psychological knowledge and its relationship to the individual. In particular, it explored psychological theories of development, language and gender, and the impact of this psychological knowledge on social practices such as racism, education and organisational assessment.

Giddens (1991) therefore explored sociological knowledge and both Rose (1985, 1990) and Henriques *et al.* (1984) focused their attention on analysing psychological knowledge. In the same way that the social studies of science studies science, these authors have studied social science. In contrast to the social studies of science, however, and its focus on scientific research, Giddens (1991), Rose (1985, 1990) and Henriques *et al.* (1984) focused on the use of social science knowledge rather than on the mechanics of its production. They examined how psychological and sociological expertise is disseminated rather than how it is created, and how social science truths are utilised by social practices rather than how these truths come to be known.

Whatever they are studying, even when studying science itself, social scientists use methodologies to produce their social science knowledge, and these methodologies could be analysed. Danziger (1990) in his book *Constructing the Subject* addressed this issue. He examined both the investigative practices of psychology such as the workings of the laboratory and the social relations of psychologists with both their subjects and other researchers. In particular, Danziger analysed research as a social practice and detailed how this social practice transformed research findings into psychological truths. His analysis focused on research up to the mid-twentieth century. In addition, it mainly analysed the experimental methodologies central to the production of psychological facts with a focus on personality research rather than facts from other aspects of psychology. It also focused solely on psychology rather than including related disciplines. What about the breadth of tools used to produce social science facts? What about the broader range of methodologies used by social scientists, their theories and their measurements? What about more recent developments?

Scientific theories have been studied but those social science theories implicit within this study are left unexplored. The initial choice of a research question, the choice of perspective, the framing of results and the production of the final research paper all require the writer to draw upon a discourse concerning a theoretical framework. Such theoretical orientations could also be examined. In line with the study of scientific methods, the methods could also be explored. The generation of interview data requires the interviewer to draw upon a discourse concerning interview technique and the production of observational data requires an understanding of the discourse on observational methods. The measurements used by social scientists also remain unstudied. For example, the production of questionnaire data requires an understanding of the discourse concerning measurement, and interviews are based upon an understanding of the discourses around the production of interview schedules. Surely, if the theories developed and tested by scientists can be analysed, so too can the theories of social scientists. If the methods used to produce scientific facts can be 'read', then those used to produce social science facts can also be read. Likewise, if the strategies used to measure scientific phenomena can be explored, so too can those used for social science phenomena. These strategies of theory, methodology and measurement constitute the disciplines of social science which themselves can be analysed as discourse. To date social science analysts of discourse have left the discourse of social science relatively unexplored. Furthermore, although turning their analysis on to the object of science, the production of the object of social science remains underanalysed.

The aim of this book

The social studies of science draws upon the literature of social science to explore the production of scientific facts. This book studies the production of social science facts. The social studies of science also explores the relationship between the discourse of science and its object; the scientific fact. This book explores the relationship between the discourse of social science and its object; the individual. Gergen (1991) argued that social psychology is inevitably a form of social history and that notions of the self change as society changes. Thomas also argued that 'Not only might the self be

> • Psychology and sociology texts as discourse
>
> • Constructing what the individual is
>
>   **(methodology, measurement and theory as constructing strategies)**
>
> • Constructing what the individual is not
>
>   **(boundaries as constructing strategies)**

Figure 1.3   The aims of this book

different in form and content in different times and countries and cultures, but the theories we produce about the self will change; they too will be a product of time and culture' (1996, p. 323). This book examines social science as a form of social history and explores the changing shape of the individual as described by the fabric of these disciplines. In particular, it examines the strategies of theory, methodology and measurement and their role in the construction of what the individual is. This book also examines how social science constructs what the individual is not. To this end it draws upon the rhetoric of these disciplines and focuses on the use of boundaries between social science and medicine and between the individual and the social (Figure 1.3).

This social study of social science focuses on the discourses of sociology and psychology. Specifically, this book examines how selected exemplar cases of sociological and psychological text illuminate the construction of the object of social science. In particular it analyses those discourses relating to health, as health offers a pivotal point for the merger of social science perspectives and provides an increasingly powerful prism through which to study the individual (Armstrong, 2002).

A note on the use of data

The aim of this book is to explore the ways in which social science discourse constructs its object. To this end the literature of social science in the form of journal articles and books is treated as primary data which can be analysed in the same way as questionnaire or interview data. Within psychology and sociology the potential data that could be scrutinised in this way are vast. Areas of research and literature have therefore been selected for analysis and exemplar cases within these areas have been chosen. The data are not randomly selected; neither can they be considered representative of all social science data, but they reflect a heterogeneous sample of papers and books to offer maximum variety. Chapter 2 through to Chapter 7 focuses on these primary data and the book draws upon the literature on health and risk (Chapter 2), sex (Chapter 3), health status (Chapter 4), and textbooks (Chapters 6 and 7). Chapters 1 and 8 reflect the positioning of the primary data within the existing literature. A further analysis of primary and secondary data can be found in Chapter 7.

2 Theory as data
The examples of health and risk

Social scientists conventionally collect data from individuals and use these data to support and develop theoretical perspectives about human beings. Whether these data are collected using quantitative or qualitative methodologies, the relationship between theory, data and the object of that theory (the individual) is considered to be relatively unproblematic. Theories are viewed as intentional constructs; they are 'about' the individual. Thus, the individual who is described by theory has an existence independent of that theory. Theoretical progress is understood in terms of an increasing approximation between the individual described by theory and the individual in reality; theory becomes more accurate. This model of science construes theory as a window through which the world is understood. However, such an unproblematic model of the relationship between theory and the individual ignores the capacity of this window to transform and distort the individual. Such a model also neglects the potential of the window to construct its object (Table 2.1).

Examination of theory within psychology through the twentieth century suggests a pattern in terms of the changing description of the individual. Similar changes may be found within medical, sociological and health care theories concerning risk. An examination of changes in these theoretical perspectives can provide insights into the way theory transforms the individual. Such an examination can also reveal changes in social science's construction of its object. In other words, theory may be treated as data and an analysis of these data can reveal the ways in which the object of social science is constructed.

Table 2.1 The roles of theory

Conventional view	Alternative view
Theory provides a framework to generate hypotheses and locate data about the individual	Theory is a strategy which constructs the individual

A changing model of the individual

Cannon (1932) placed stress within a stimulus/response framework and emphasised the importance of characteristics of the world external to the individual. Half a century later, Lazarus (Lazarus and Cohen, 1977) redefined stress as a transaction between the individual and the external world. Stress was still conceptualised within a stimulus/response framework but the individual was characterised as an active, perceiving, appraising information processor who interacted with the outside world. This shift from passive responder to interactive appraiser indicates a fundamental trans-formation of the object of psychological thought. Moreover, many psycho-logical theories, although presented as independent of each other, illustrate the same reconfiguration of the essence of the individual over a comparable time period. This chapter examines this changing alignment between the individual and their environment and argues that the last decades of the twentieth century marked the appearance of a novel psychological object which finds reflection in sociological, medical and health care theories of risk.

The passive identity

At the beginning of the twentieth century a number of psychological theories emerged which described the individual as a passive responder to external events. For example, early researchers such as Pavlov (1927) and Skinner (1953) analysed the effects of external stimuli on individual behaviour in terms of operant and classical conditioning. Operant conditioning research examined reinforcement and the effects of these external processes on increasing or decreasing the probability of the recurrence of the behaviour. Theories of classical conditioning suggested that a conditioned response would occur when the unconditioned stimuli had been sufficiently paired with the conditioned stimuli. Such stimulus/response models considered the individual as being shaped and acted on by external events.

In a similar fashion, early models of addiction also characterised the psychological object as being the recipient of external action. The redefini-tion of alcoholism from a moral issue to a disease – as conceptualised by the first disease model – emphasised the addictive nature of the substance in use. Within this framework alcohol was regarded as having distinct and dangerous characteristics and the addict was seen as an unfortunate victim. This perspective created a suitable environment for national prohibition in America and a decline in the status of such addictive substances in Britain. The early twentieth-century addict was influenced and created by their exterior world.

Early models of stress and pain also reproduced the same psychological configuration. Theories of stress suggested that stress was a response to an external stressor (Cannon, 1932; Seyle, 1956). Cannon (1932) analysed stress in terms of the fight/flight dyad which conceptualised stress as a survival response to external threats. Selye later developed the General Adaptation Syndrome which assumed a consistency in this stress response in terms of 'physiological arousal' and predicted that prolonged stimulus together with the release of stress hormones could result in physical damage and illness (Seyle, 1956). In a similar vein, pain was described as a response to physical damage caused by an external stimulus. Von Frey (1895) developed the specificity theory of pain which posited the existence of specific sensory receptors to transmit touch, warmth and pain. This suggested a similar stimulus/response model of the individual to that proposed by Goldschneider's contemporary pattern theory of pain (1920).

In summary, in the first half of the twentieth century a number of psychological models, including theories of behaviour, addiction, stress and pain, focused attention on the external cue as the factor responsible for the individual's response. Individual behaviour was seen as a reaction to circumstances outside the body and individual identity was characterised by passivity and the absence of agency (Figure 2.1).

Figure 2.1   The passive responder

The interactive identity

From the 1960s a more animated object began to appear in psychological theory. Learning theorists continued to analyse behaviour in terms of mechanisms such as operant and classical conditioning, but began to emphasise an interactive alignment of the individual and their environment. Theorists such as Rescorla and Wagner (1972), Pearce and Hall (1980), Mackintosh (1974) and Dickinson (1980) reaffirmed the traditional laws of conditioning but argued that it was also important to incorporate the cognitions and processing capacity of the individual. Learning was therefore analysed in terms of types of mental representations and stimulus characteristics; individuals were characterised by their ability to process information.

At the same time social learning theorists were also evaluating the mechanisms of behaviour. Consistent with earlier theories, reinforcement and modelling were regarded as important determinants of the individual's behaviour. However, the individual was not conceptualised as being shaped by external stimuli but as an interactive processor of these same stimuli. For example, in the early 1960s, Bandura's classic experiments on aggression examined the effect of modelling on shaping childhood aggression in the context of debate about which characteristics of the aggressor were pertinent to the child (Bandura *et al.*, 1963). Within this framework, behaviour was conceptualised as being mediated by selective processing and as a product of interactions between individuals, and between the individual and the outside world. The individual was characterised by an increasing sense of agency.

Contemporaneously, social psychologists developed models to explain health behaviours such as eating, smoking, drinking and screening which reproduced the reconfiguration of the relationship of the individual to their environment. The health belief model (HBM), first defined in the 1960's (Becker, 1974; Rosenstock, 1966) examined factors which might predict health behaviours. The model conceptualised external events as cues to action which were perceived and appraised by the individual. The health belief model also examined the interrelationship between the individual and their environment in terms of an interplay between cognitions and the external world which was operationalised as perceived severity and perceived preventability of the resulting ill health. Health behaviours, far from being a response to external stimuli, were a consequence of this interrelationship.

A similar pattern is also illustrated by models of addiction. The second disease concept of addiction, developed by Jellinek in 1960, placed an increasing importance on the characteristics of the individual. Addiction was seen as arising either from a pre-existing physical abnormality or a pre-existing psychological abnormality. This perspective no longer emphasised the characteristics of the addictive substance but introduced the active individual into the equation. As with contemporary models of eating behaviour the individual was conceptualised as interacting with the substance. This focus on interaction was further developed within the self-control model of addiction (Heather and Robertson, 1979; Marlatt and Gordon, 1980) which emphasised social learning in the acquisition of an addictive behaviour. Conditioning processes such as modelling and reinforcement and the selective processing of external stimuli were seen as responsible for developing an addictive behaviour.

Theories of stress and pain also focused increasingly on an interplay between the individual and their environment. Lazarus' transactional analysis of stress in 1977 (Lazarus and Cohen, 1977) introduced the concept of appraisal and suggested that individuals appraised stressors as either benign or threatening and that this appraisal determined the extent of the stress response. In addition, Lazarus argued that individuals appraised their available coping responses. This accentuation of appraisal processes indicated that stress was no longer conceptualised as a response to external threat but as a result of the individuals' perceptions and their ability to cope with the stressor. As a result of Lazarus' transactional analysis of stress, research emphasised the interplay between individual factors and an

Figure 2.2   The interactive individual

external threat and attempted to characterise elements of the external threat that were selectively processed. This pattern can also be seen with the gate control theory of pain (Melzack, 1979; Melzack and Wall, 1965, 1982) which focused on the individuals' previous experience and interpretations of the meaning and experience of pain.

In summary, a major shift in the identity of the individual emerged in a number of psychological theories from the 1960s (Figure 2.2). In essence, the individual was conceptualised as an interactive being who processed information from the environment. Research emphasised perception about external stimuli whether these were cues to action, reinforcers, life events, the addictive substance, the stressor or the painful stimuli. Within this interactive framework, behaviour, stress and pain were construed as intentional constructs – as being about something in the external world. Whereas during the first half of the twentieth century psychology outlined the passive responder in theories of human behaviour, the later years marked the emergence of a new active and interactive agent: the object of psychological thought was emerging as the subjective self.

The transformation in the construction of individual identity could be regarded as a progression towards revealing the true nature of identity – an interactive, appraising active being. However, in the last decades of the twentieth century there was evidence of an additional transformation of the object of psychology as a new alignment between the individual and the environment began to emerge.

The intra-active identity

When the health belief model was first developed, researchers applied it to a variety of behaviours including smoking, eating, breast and cervical screening and exercise (Becker and Rosenstock, 1984; Hill *et al.*, 1985; Janz and Becker, 1984). At first, critics of the HBM suggested that it ignored symptom perception, that it presented a rational information-processing model of individuals and that it had been inconsistently operationalised (Leventhal and Nerenz, 1985; Winett, 1985). However, the main recent criticism of the HBM is that it does not include self-efficacy – the confidence that the desired behaviour can be carried out – and as a result the HBM has been reformulated to include this variable (Becker and Rosenstock, 1987; Rosenstock *et al.*, 1988).

Self-efficacy was first defined by Bandura in 1977 and has since been applied to a wide range of both health- and non-health-related behaviours (Bandura, 1977, 1986, 1988, 1989, 1990, 1991; Bandura *et al.*, 1985). The concept of self-efficacy suggested that individuals evaluate the extent to which they can control their own behaviour given particular situations. For example, the Protection Motivation Theory (PMT) (Rogers, 1983) focused on threat appraisal (severity and vulnerability) and response effectiveness to predict behavioural intentions and consequently behaviour, but in addition emphasised the role of self-efficacy in predicting behaviour and attitude change. This emphasis placed the focus of behavioural change on the individual's ability to master their own behaviour. In his book *Self Efficacy: Thought Control of Action* Schwarzer (1992) reviewed the research into health behaviours and claimed that self-efficacy was consistently the best predictor of behavioural intentions and behaviour change for a variety of behaviours such as the intention to floss, frequency of flossing, effective use of contraception, breast self-examination, intention to use clean needles, intention to quit smoking, and intention to adhere to weight loss programmes and exercise (Beck and Lund, 1981; Becker and Avard, 1986; Dzewaltowski, 1989; Gilchrist and Schinke, 1983; Kok *et al.*, 1990; Seydal *et al.*, 1990). Schwarzer's own model of health behaviour, the Health Action Process Approach (HAPA) placed self-efficacy within the context of self-regulatory processes, outcome expectancies and threat appraisal. Schwarzer argued that 'self efficacy determines the amount of effort invested and the perseverance' (1992, p. 237) and suggested that, compared to all the factors in the HAPA, self-efficacy was the best predictor of behaviour.

The emphasis on self-efficacy as a predictor of behaviour indicates a recent reconfiguration of the relationship between the individual and their environment. The individual is no longer conceptualised as passively responding to external cues, nor as interacting with their environment, but as interacting with their own inner self.

A similar shift can also be seen in the literature on addiction. Contemporary models of addictive behaviour now emphasise self-control in the maintenance of abstinence or controlled behaviour (Marlatt and Gordon, 1985). Within this framework, behaviour is determined by the factors located within the individual. This shift is epitomised by Marlatt and Gordon's model of relapse prevention developed in 1985. According to this theory, if an individual is attempting to abstain from an addictive behaviour, and is challenged by a high-risk situation, the probability of relapse is determined by their degree of self-control. The model suggested that low self-efficacy and an internal attribution for a lapse predicted a full-blown relapse whereas high self-efficacy and external attributions will predict a return to abstinence. Marlatt and Gordon introduced the concept of 'maintenance man' and argued that the individual becomes the 'agent of change'. In effect, as with models of health behaviour, self-efficacy is conceptualised as the main determinant of behaviour. Within the framework of the self-control model of addiction, the determinant of behaviour is no longer the external substance nor the individual's interaction with that substance but the individual's inner self. This inner self is construed in its turn as changeable, and something to be mastered and managed by the individual's self-efficacy.

A parallel pattern has also emerged in the stress and pain literature. In recent years the characteristics of the external stressor have played a diminishing role in the transaction between the individual and their environment and the individualised factors have been conceptualised as increasingly important. For example, Lazarus and Folkman (1987) suggested that self-efficacy was a powerful resource for coping with stress. Moreover, research also indicated that self-efficacy may influence stress-mediated immune function (Wiedenfeld *et al.*, 1990), and that if confronted with a threatening situation, self-efficacy influences responses in terms of blood pressure, heart rate and the release of stress hormones (Bandura *et al.*, 1982, 1985, 1988). In addition, reports have claimed that self-efficacy influences recovery from heart attacks (Taylor *et al.*, 1985). The new models of stress no longer encompass an interplay between the self and the external stressor as suggested by Lazarus' original transactional model, but a reflexive interplay between the self and the self. Comparative patterns can also be seen in the recent pain literature with the emphasis shifting to the central control component and the concept of pain locus of control (Dolce, 1987; Litt, 1988; Manning and Wright, 1983). The stress response and the pain experience also became located within the individual, and the presence, or degree, of this response/experience is determined by the individual's ability to control themselves.

Taken together, models of health behaviour such as the redefined HBM, the PMT and the HAPA point to a shift in perspective in psychological theory in terms of causes of behaviour and the relationship between the individual and their environment. It is no longer conditioning processes and associations arising from external cues that shape behaviour, nor the inter-actions between the individual and the external world. Instead behaviour is conceptualised as a consequence of the individual's ability to control and determine their own behaviour – their self-efficacy. In a similar vein, con-temporary stress and pain models examine coping and self-control, and addictive behaviour is considered as arising from the individual presence or absence of self-control.

In summary, there were two major transformations in the object of psychology during the twentieth century which were reproduced in the changing alignment between the individual and the environment. The first occurred in the 1960s when the passive identity of the body who was shaped by external cues became the interactive identity as the individual was conceptualised as processing information from the environment. Indi-viduals were increasingly typified by their agency and their cognition, but the environment was still an important factor in the interactive process. The

Figure 2.3   The intra-active individual

human mind was governed by intentionality and was characterised by an 'aboutness' directed to an extra-corporal world. However, in the last decades of the twentieth century, a second transformation occurred in which the environment was largely removed from the equation. Individuals still possess agency and are characterised by their 'aboutness' but this is no longer directed outside the body. The contemporary intra-active individual is characterised by an agency and an intentionality which is directed internally towards their inner self. The late twentieth-century object of psychological thought became a subjective entity whose subject was the self (Figure 2.3).

Risks to health

The mutation from passivity through interaction to the intra-active identity parallels changing concepts of risks to health over the century. Early biomedical models of health and illness explained the individual's health to be at risk from external influences. Illnesses were understood to be caused by organic and environmental factors such as viruses, bacteria and pollution which sometimes successfully penetrated the body's defence mechanisms. Such threats to health were conceptualised as separate and outside the fixed constitution of the body. The body of the patient was seen as a passive object which was shaped by external forces. Within this framework risk perception involved evaluating external risks to health.

In 1977, Engel argued that the biomedical model should be expanded to include the psychosocial as in a biopsychosocial model of health and illness (Engel, 1977, 1980). This perspective generated research into the interaction between the individual (bio and psycho) and the external world (social). The literature emphasised the role of behaviour, cognition and perception. As in contemporary psychological theories, the individual was conceptualised as an interactive being who appraised and perceived their external world. Risk perception involved assessing risks to health which arose from this interaction.

More recently the concept of health risk has changed again. The risk is no longer external to the self in the form of viruses and pollution as in biomedical models, nor a product of interactions between the individual and their environment as in the biopsychosocial model. The risk to health is conceptualised as an internal, malleable and manageable self. The risk to health comes from the individual's presence or absence of self-control which manages and masters the changeable drives that expose the body to threats. The HIV virus itself is no longer a risk to health: the individual's ability to control their sexual behaviour is now the risk. Diseases such as cervical cancer do not constitute a risk to health in themselves but reflect the individual's ability to have regular screening and to take preventive action. Equally, the risk of addiction is seen in terms of self-control and self-efficacy, and stress and pain research illustrates a shift towards individual control over their experience. In the late twentieth century the individual became at risk from his or herself.

Risk and social theory

In an analysis of the contemporary location of risk, Beck, in his book *The Risk Society* (1986), emphasised the role of technology, industrialised society and pollution in the constitution of risk and located risk as existing in the environment. He discussed the concept of 'victimisation by risks' (p. 41) and claimed that in a developed civilisation 'a new global ascription of risks [is emerging] against which individual decisions hardly exist' (p. 41). Within Beck's model the individual is construed as being passively at risk from environmental hazards.

An alternative model of risk in the late twentieth century has been given by Armstrong in 1993 in his development of Douglas' thesis *Purity and Danger* (Douglas, 1966). Douglas defined the concept of 'dirt' as matter out of place, and argued that rules of hygiene were a means of separating polluted spaces from healthy spaces. Within this framework a risk to health is the object which threatens to cross the boundary between spaces. Armstrong extended Douglas' analysis of hygiene rules to describe the changing configuration of the boundaries between medicalised spaces over the past two centuries in terms of four models of public health spaces. These models have implications for understanding both the changing conceptualisations of risks to health and the changing identity of the individual.

Armstrong described the 'quarantine model' of hygiene whereby lines were drawn between healthy and unhealthy spaces such as houses, towns or ships. Within this context, risks to health were located in places. He argued that 'illness somehow resided in places, as it was places that had to be kept separate' (p. 3). The next model of hygiene emerged in the mid-nineteenth century in the form of 'sanitary science'. This was concerned with monitoring the passage of substances such as air, water, faeces and semen across the boundary of the body. The focus on sewage, and air and water pollution apparent in the late nineteenth century, identified risks to health as located between 'the space of the body and non-corporal external space'. Within this model risks to health were characterised by a physical exchange between the body and the outside world. The third model of 'personal hygiene' appeared early in the twentieth century. It represented a focus on personal cleanliness and behaviours such as exercise, eating and smoking. Within this framework risks to health were located within a space defined by 'the boundaries between people', and the individual's health status was threatened by their interactions with other individuals.

The final contemporary model of hygiene described by Armstrong is that of the new public health. He argued that late twentieth-century hygiene rules no longer conceptualised risks to health as existing in places, nor in objects that cross the boundary of the body nor the interpersonal space of the social. Instead the contemporary emphasis on health promotion, lifestyle, and the 'green response' to ecological dangers located risks to health as existing everywhere. Within this framework, risks to health exist in the spaces between individuals and each other and between individuals and the socially engineered environment. This shift to the idea that risks are located everywhere constitutes a form of surveillance, which, following Foucault (1979b), reconfigures the individual 'through their constant and pervasive observation' (p. 14).

However, perhaps the contemporary health risks are neither located in the environment nor in the spaces produced by interpersonal interactions with this environment but, as indicated by the contemporary psychological literature, are to be found within the self. It is true that the health promotion movement of the late twentieth century focused on lifestyle, as suggested by Armstrong, but the movement emphasises personal control over lifestyle. The movement is also concerned with environmental pollutants, as suggested by Beck, but the emphasis is on personal control over emitting these pollutants. Health promotion encourages safe sex, healthy eating, screening, smoking and drug abstinence and alcohol moderation. All such behaviour changes involve activating self-control and using this self-control to modify risk. In addition, the proliferation of self-help groups, relaxation tapes, screening and the new genetics all subscribe to the concept of 'being at risk from yourself' and the activation of internal resources to reduce this risk. Therefore, both theories of risk and the resulting practical manifestation of these theories are further illustrations of the process of reconfiguring the individual as intra-active and of the relocation of risks to health as existing within the self; the creation of the risky self (Ogden, 1995a, 1995b) (Figure 2.4).

Theory and its object

To conclude, theoretical models within psychology illustrate a shift in their descriptions of their object (the individual) from one who passively responds to their environment, to one who interacts with it, to, most recently, one who is increasingly intra-active. Theories about risk from sociology, medicine and health care practices indicate shifts parallel to psychology in their reconfiguration of their model of the individual with the

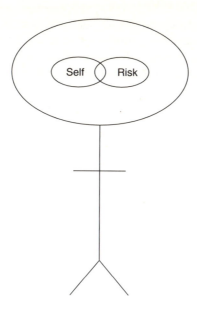

Figure 2.4 The risky self

construction of the risky self. Therefore, contemporary theories across many disciplinary discourses describe an individual who is intra-active and risks to health which are located within the individual. If theory is seen to describe its object, then theories within these apparently disparate theories can be said to be describing an ever-changing object. If theory and its object are seen as interdependent, then the theories of psychology, medicine and health care can be seen as transforming their object. However, if a more problematic relationship between theory and its object is taken, then the changing theories of the individual seen within psychology, medical and health care practices are not describing or transforming their object but constructing it. As the theories change so does their object. The theories of these disciplines are not windows which describe or transform their object but strategies which create and construct their object.

Towards a social study of social science . . .

The social study of science explores the ways in which scientific discourse constructs the object of this discourse, the scientific fact. This chapter has explored how one aspect of social science constructs the object of social science. Although theory is often considered a strategy to reveal and understand the individual, this chapter has illustrated how it can also be a strategy for the construction of the individual. As theories of the individual change, so does the individual, and over the past one hundred years this individual has transformed from a passive entity to one who is intra-active and increasingly detached from the social world. But theory is not a discipline's only constructive strategy. The methods used to collect and analyse data and the process of sample selection are also central to the transformation of the self. Methodology is the focus of the next chapter.

3   Methodology as data

The example of sex research

Books and papers have analysed theories about sexual practice from within a range of different perspectives as a means to address the 'nature' of sexuality. For example, from a feminist psychological perspective, Segal (1994) suggested that contemporary theories about sex remain biomedical in their reductionist approach and construct sex as biological. She argued that in contrast to this approach, sex should be seen as power. From a sociological perspective Weeks (1985) emphasised a need to study modern sexualities, and in particular focused on changing representations of sexualities and the important role of the unconscious. In contrast, Holland *et al.* (1990a) explored the gendered power relations inherent within descriptions of sex, and historians such as Porter and Hall (1995) have provided a detailed description of the history of sexual knowledge. Each different analysis varies in the extent to which it problematises the relationship between theory and its object and the extent to which it argues that theories of sexuality either describe, interpret or construct their sexual object. The relationship between theory and its object was addressed in the previous chapter. The methodologies used to generate and test theories within key studies of sexual behaviour are the focus of this chapter.

Methodology is conventionally regarded as a tool to collect data. However, not only can the theories produced by methodology be studied, but the methodologies themselves can be examined as strategies to construct the individual (Table 3.1). This perspective is suggested by Foucault in his *History of Sexuality* (1979a, 1981, p. 79) by his tale of Diderot and the magic of Diderot's ring:

> In Diderot's tale, the good genie Cucufa discovers . . . the tiny silver ring whose stone, when turned, makes the sexes one encounters speak. . . . It is this magical ring, this jewel which is so indiscreet when it comes to making others speak, but so ineloquent concerning its own mechanism . . . We must write the history of this will to truth.

Foucault therefore argued that it is not only the stories that are revealed by the ring which tell the 'truth' but also the changing nature of the ring itself.

Table 3.1 The roles of methodology

Conventional view	*Alternative view*
Methodology is a tool to collect data about the individual	Methodology is a strategy to construct the individual

In the case of psychology and sociology the ring represents the methodologies used to describe and find out the truth about the individual.

Over the twentieth century, research used both qualitative methods involving in-depth interviews and the analysis of text and quantitative methods involving structured interviews, questionnaires, laboratory observation or experimentation. At varying times such methodologies have been accompanied by concerns for issues such as researcher bias, sampling, accuracy of subject response, the importance of fact and the importance of experience. These methodologies have been used to examine the nature of sexual behaviour and can be analysed by asking the questions 'what methods are used?', 'who is the sample and how is it accessed?' and 'how are the results analysed and presented?' These questions will be applied to the study of sexual behaviour over the twentieth century as a means to explore changes in methodology and to examine methodology as a strategy for constructing its object; the individual (Figure 3.1).

- What methods are used?
- Who is the sample?
- How are the results analysed and presented?

Figure 3.1 Studying methodology

Methods of the early twentieth century

At the beginning of the twentieth century, writings placed sexual behaviour firmly within the context of reproduction and regarded behaviours such as homosexuality, contraception and masturbation which were not concerned with reproduction as immoral and abnormal. Research into sexual behaviour was rare and texts describing sexual behaviour were inaccessible to the majority. In fact many writings were of limited publication to actually reduce their accessibility. For example, Bloch (1909) opened his book *The Sexual Life of our Time* with the statement that the book was to be

> limited to members of the legal and medical professions. . . . To both these professions it is essential that a knowledge of the science of sex

and the various causes for the existence of 'abnormals' should be ascertained, so that they may be guided in the future in their investigations into, and the practice of attempts to mitigate, the evil which undoubtedly exists and to bring about a more healthy class of beings.

What methods were used? Perhaps the most well-known individual working in the area of sexuality at the beginning of the century was Freud with his theories of repression, symbolism and the unconscious. Freud based his theories upon his own clinical practice as a therapist. When describing the development of his theories Freud emphasised the role of experience and stated that 'the accumulated impressions from which we derive our theories could be arrived at in no other way' (Freud, 1933, p. 187). When discussing the validity of psychoanalysis as a method of treatment Freud argued that rather than relying upon statistics or large samples, 'it is wiser to examine one's individual experiences' (Freud, 1933, p. 187). This approach is also shown by other early workers in this field. For example, Forel and Marshall (1908) in their book *The Sexual Question* described sexual behaviour and attempted to provide a framework for normality and abnormality. They stated that 'This book is the fruit of long experience and reflection'. Likewise, Bloch (1909) wrote extensively about heterosexual intercourse but, when describing female homosexuality, simply stated, 'I do not know what actually occurs in practice'. Similarly Von Krafft-Ebbing in his writings on perversion and abnormality presented his own professional views on what was acceptable behaviour and then illustrated his ideas with case histories of attenders at Austrian courts (Von Krafft-Ebbing, 1894).

The literature around this time therefore relied upon professional experience as its methodology. For many writers their professional beliefs remained implicit. However, some, such as Stopes (1926), who wrote 'our sex life is our most direct link with the Divine life', involved the explicit presentation of professional beliefs. In addition, some writers not only clearly expressed their professional beliefs but dictated how such beliefs should be communicated to others. Stopes provided a good example of this in her text *Sex and the Young* (1926, pp. 168–70) when she wrote,

> when as a mother or father you are with your children it is vital to be most careful to answer truly. . . . The very first time the query comes 'Mother where did you get me?' the mother must not divert the child's interest or hesitate, but should be ready at once to answer: 'God and daddy and I together made you because we wanted you'. 'Did God help. Couldn't He do it all by himself?' . . . God thought Daddy and Mummy would like him to help, but not to do everything, because Daddy and Mummy enjoyed making you more than you enjoy playing with bricks.

Theories at the beginning of the twentieth century described sex as biological, sex for reproduction and sex within a moral framework. However,

• What methods are used?	Professional experience
• Who is the sample?	A clinical minority
• How are the results presented and analysed?	As facts with comment

Figure 3.2   Methods of the early twentieth century

the methodologies used to elicit these theories also tell a story. Truths about sexuality were produced using the methods of insight and experience which were not those of just anyone but of professionals whose insights were given authority by their experience, qualifications or by the highest authority: God. If evidence was sought it was only to support the facts which were already known. Others were only occasionally called upon to provide illustrations for such expert views, and the results of this analysis were presented uncritically as the truth (Figure 3.2).

The methods of the mid-twentieth century

Research exploring sexual behaviour in the mid-twentieth century reveals a shift in emphasis. Sex was still generally considered within a biological framework but texts were no longer concerned with sex for reproduction but with sex for pleasure. The outcome of sex was studied in terms of sexual desire, pleasure and orgasms, and this resulted in a burgeoning literature on sex therapy and produced manuals on how to have a good sex life. This emphasis was first illustrated by the works of Kinsey (1948, 1953) who wrote two books entitled *Sexual Behaviour in the Human Male* and *Sexual Behaviour in the Human Female* and developed his analysis within the framework of biological reductionism. In particular, he argued that sex was natural, that the sexual drive was a biological force and therefore that the desire to have sex was not only natural but desirable. He also indicated that a variety of sexual outlets were acceptable, that a healthy sex life could lead to healthy and happy marriages and emphasised the importance of sexual pleasure for both men and women involving both masturbation and sexual intercourse. His work stirred America and challenged existing beliefs about sex, marriage and the family.

What methods did he use? Kinsey adhered to the scientific method in terms of his methods of data collection, his choice of sample and his approach to data analysis. For data collection, Kinsey used case histories derived from in-depth face-to-face interviews which are described as 'fact finding sessions in which the interviewer and the subject have found equal satisfaction in exploring the accumulated record'. Kinsey showed concern for researcher bias and the 'objectivity of the investigator'. He described how each interview commenced with a confirmation that the interviewer 'was not passing judgement on any type of sexual activity' and how the interviewer used an 'objective manner', a 'simple directness of his questions' and a 'failure to show any emotional objection to any part of the record'. He also used a range of interviewers to account for individual interview styles. His research used methods which illustrated a concern for impartiality, interview bias, deceit and accuracy; in fact he clearly described his work as a 'fact finding survey' (Kinsey *et al.*, 1948). He described his motivation for carrying out his research as resulting from the difficulty in obtaining 'strictly factual information which was not biased by moral, philosophic or social interpretations' (Kinsey *et al.*, 1948, p. 5) and argued that he managed to collect so much data 'by guaranteeing the confidence of the record, and by abstaining from judgements or attempts to redirect the behaviour of any of the subjects' (Kinsey *et al.*, 1953, p. 7).

He also expressed a determination to gather truthful and reliable data from his subjects. For example, he emphasised the interviewer's ability to 'check the honesty of the response' by an examination of the subject's 'tone of voice, the direction of his eye, the intonation and the directness of circumlocution of his statement . . . [to] provide a clue to the quality of the information which he is giving'. He stated that the interviewer could ask additional questions to check for consistency and truthfulness and that the reliability of the data was tested by 'securing retakes of histories from subjects who had previously given us histories' and comparing the interview transcripts for the two time points. He described how the data were also checked for validity by comparing the responses from spouses when describing the same sexual act. To supplement his case histories Kinsey used data sources such as correspondence, sexual calendars and diaries, art materials, community observation studies and previously published works. Much of this work was also used to test the validity of the case histories by comparing the types of data collected using the different methodologies.

For his sample, Kinsey involved nearly 17,000 white American men and women following his determination to collect data from as wide a sample as possible which could then be made 'available to the maximum number of persons'. He detailed the problems with probability sampling and described the method used as group sampling which enabled the researchers to secure representatives of a range of larger groups. Kinsey and his co-workers sampled according to social units including prisons, armed forces, clinical groups, college classes, church organisations and business office groups. Their sample was then presented in terms of demographic factors such as age range, educational background, marital status, religious background, class and geographical origin. Finally, in terms of actual data analysis, all case histories were recorded using a box-checking method and these data were analysed directly, again reducing the possibility of bias.

Therefore, his methods of collecting data illustrated a substantial concern for fact finding, bias, accuracy and the scientific method. In particular, he expressed concern over 'contamination' of the data from both the researcher and the participant. His approach to sampling reflected a desire to collect data which were generalisable and representative of the population at large. Finally, how were the results presented? Throughout the descriptions of his findings Kinsey offered interpretation and comment and located his results within the salient social issues of the time. For example, he linked his findings on homosexual activity to the legal status of this behaviour, stating, 'the judge who is considering the case of the male who has been arrested for homosexual activity, should keep in mind that nearly 40 per cent of all the other males in the town could be arrested at some time in their lives for similar activity' (Kinsey *et al.*, 1948, p. 664). He also provided a detailed analysis of the possible reasons for sexual contact with animals and suggested that 'the easy dismissal of such behaviour by characterising it as abnormal shows little capacity for making objective analyses of the basic psychology that is involved' (1948, p. 675). He was also critical of psychiatrists (particularly from Europe) who 'look upon masturbation in the history of the married male as nothing short of pathologic' and suggested that 'this is of course, merely a rationalisation of their own European mores' (1948, p. 675). Kinsey therefore collected his data from large samples, he checked for researcher bias and assessed the reliability and validity of the accounts given. He then presented his findings along with an interpretation of their implications for society as a whole.

Following closely on from the Kinsey reports was the work of Masters and Johnson (1966, 1970). They were interested in the biological mechanisms of sexual intercourse, emphasised the similarities between men and women and published works entitled *The Human Sexual Response* (1966) and *Human Sexual Inadequacy* (1970). In particular, they described the sexual response cycle in terms of the stages of excitement, plateau, orgasm and resolution and argued that sexual pleasures could be improved by education and sex therapy, and focused on sex for pleasure and sex as an essential component of a stable marriage.

What methods did Masters and Johnson use? Masters and Johnson collected their data in the laboratory under controlled conditions and focused on quantifiable physiological and anatomical responses including heart rate, muscle tension, changes in shape and colour of the sexual organs, degree of lubrication, frequency and length of contractions, breast changes and respiratory responses. To collect their data they asked volunteers either to masturbate under observation in the laboratory by hand, fingers, or using a mechanical vibrator or to have heterosexual sexual intercourse in a variety of positions with a partner or with a transparent probe. All measurements were taken using either externally attached tools or miniaturised cameras and electronic devises placed inside a plastic phallus to take recordings internally. In terms of sampling, their studies involved the participation of 694 individuals including 276 married couples and 142 unmarried individuals, of whom forty-four had been married in the past. The men ranged in age from 21 to 89 and the women ranged from 18 to 78. They also included seven women aged between 19 and 34 who had been born without a vagina. They therefore did not attempt to use any precise sampling method to ensure that their method was representative of the population at large. However, in line with the sampling methods employed by laboratory research they assumed that biological factors would be similar between individuals and therefore opted for a hetero-geneous sample to provide a range of responses. Their data were then analysed by simply examining the responses recorded by their machinery.

For their data collection, sampling and data analysis Masters and Johnson adhered to the scientific method. So how were their results pre-sented? Like Kinsey's, the descriptions of their findings involved comment and interpretation. For example, although they only took measurements in the laboratory they extrapolated from their results to make conclusions about relationships, and in particular the state of marriage in the USA. They argued that 'the greatest single cause [of divorce] is a fundamental sexual inadequacy within the marital unit' (1966, p. vi) and played a fundamental part in the marketing of sex manuals to promote good sex as a means of maintaining successful marriages. Therefore, they adhered to the scientific method in terms of data collection and the use of large samples. They presented their results with comment and interpretation.

In contrast to earlier research with its focus on professional experience and authority, the use of both case histories and laboratory work in the mid-twentieth century illustrated a focus on the scientific method as the mode for producing truths about sex. The methodologies both of Kinsey and Masters and Johnson represented an attempt to remove all bias from sex research and to examine sexual behaviour either in terms of self-report or physiological recordings from as 'pure' a perspective as possible. In particular, they aimed to remove the biases of both the researcher and the subjects being researched. Therefore, the scientific method was in operation. However, the results were presented in the context of comment and interpretation (Figure 3.3).

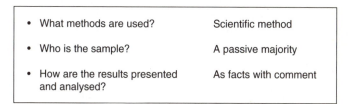

Figure 3.3   Methods of the mid-twentieth century

The transitional period

In the late 1970s and early 1980s Shere Hite published her reports on male and female sexuality entitled *The Hite Reports* (1976, 1981, 1987). As with

Kinsey and Masters and Johnson, Hite emphasised sex as pleasure and as a process rather than for reproduction. But in contrast to these previous works Hite examined a wider range of sexual experiences from love, relationships, marriage, fidelity and infidelity and friendship to orgasms in general, differences between vaginal and clitoral orgasms and preferences for penetrative or non-penetrative sex. She provided the reports from 7239 men aged from 13 to 97 and 4500 women ranging in age from under 18 to over 85 (details of exact numbers do not appear to be available).

What methodologies did Hite use? At the end of *Women and Love*, the essay on the methodologies used included commentaries from a range of authors on the contextual relevance of Hite's methodological approach. For example, Lemisch stated 'The Hite reports are part of an international trend in the social sciences expressing dissatisfaction with the adequacy of a simple quantitative method as a way of exploring people's attitudes. More and more the social sciences are turning to various qualitative methods' (Hite, 1987, p. 769). Haakinson commented that 'The research methods of the Hite Reports pioneered many current research trends, including the mixing of quantitative and qualitative data' (ibid.). Hite then provided some details of the methods used to collect data and of her sampling. In terms of data collection, Hite provided the questionnaires in appendices at the end of her work. She described how the questionnaires developed and changed over the course of her research following feedback from the respondents, and highlighted how she chose to use open-ended questions rather than multiple-choice answers which would have "told" the respondent what the allowable or normal answers would be' (Hite, 1987, p. 775). For example, her questionnaire included items on love such as 'What is the difference between being "in love" and loving someone?' She asked about the current relationship, 'How does your partner act to you in intimate moments?' and about sexuality with questions such as 'Which is the easiest way for you to orgasm?' She also enquired about identity with questions such as 'What qualities make a man a man?' With her choice of open questions, Hite showed an awareness of researcher bias and argued that 'all researchers, no matter how careful or aware/unaware of their own biases do have a point of view, a way of seeing the world, reflecting the cultural mileau in which they were brought up' (ibid.), and therefore justified her choice of method and questions as a means of minimising this bias. She was also concerned that the participants should be able to speak the truth. She stated that respondents were encouraged to write their 'thoughts and opinions on these subjects now, as well as anything else you might like to add' and to provide their answers either on paper or on tape. In fact she emphasised the use of her essay answers as a means to enable women to talk 'about their own experiences in their own voices' (1987, p. 776).

For her sampling, Hite was concerned that all responses should be anonymous, and therefore opted for the use of questionnaires which were sent to 'as many kinds of women, with as many varied points of view as possible' (1987). These were recruited by sending batches of questionnaires to organisations rather than individuals including 'church groups in 34 states, women's voting and political groups in 9 states, women's rights organisations in 39 states, professional women's groups in 22 states' for the study of women. For her study on men, Hite's aim was again to reach 'men of all ages, in all areas of the country, in all walks of life and with all outlooks and points of view' (1981, p. 1055). She then briefly described how the questionnaire was sent to 'university groups, church groups and men's discussion groups' and was printed in its entirety in a magazine entitled *Sexology* for male readers to complete and return. She provided a discussion of the representativeness of her sample and argued that it would not have been possible to use a random or stratified sample due to concerns about anonymity. However, she answered the rhetorical question 'Does research that is not based on a probability or random sample give one the right to generalise from the results of the study to the population at large?' (1987, p. 778) with the answer 'If a study is large enough and the sample broad enough and if one generalises carefully, yes' (1987, p. 778). However, she did note that no one can ever really generalise completely when measuring psychological variables as, although the data may be representative in terms of age and income, the data may not be generalisable in terms of psychological makeup. She therefore attempted to provide information from a large sample to allow some generalisations but was aware of the weaknesses of her approach.

The Hite Reports therefore showed a concern for minimising the researchers' contamination of the data and for accessing the respondents' own views and experiences. However, a different perspective is reflected in her descriptions of data analysis in an 'interactive framework'. She wanted to present the views of the interviewees themselves and argued that at times in her work 'participants debate with each other, in their own words' (1987, p. 780). In addition, she aimed to interpret what people say and indicated that 'analysis of what people are saying can bring out several possible sides of a point; researcher and participant can agree or debate at different places in the text' (1987, p. 780). She argued that 'most basic to the methodology of the Hite reports is the separation of findings from analysis and interpretation' (p. 780) and that as 'people's statements do not speak for themselves . . . it is necessary for the researcher to add an analysis and interpretation of her own'. Therefore her approach to analysis involved the views of both the participant and the researcher.

By collecting data from large numbers, in common with work of the middle of the twentieth century, Hite aimed to generate data which was generalisable. By encouraging researchers to be aware of their own perspectives and by using open questions to encourage the participants to speak freely, she illustrated a concern for researcher bias and the reliability and validity of the accounts given. In the main, however, the methodology of Hite was different to previous researchers. The laboratory science of Masters and Johnson and the determination to remove all interviewer bias found in Kinsey reflected an attempt to objectify the researcher and collect 'factual' data through the scientific method. In contrast, Hite described biases as inherent to research and facilitated the emergence of this bias by the use of interpretation as part of the analysis. Furthermore, the earlier focus on the authorial voice of the professional, Kinsey's use of closed questions and tests of reliability and validity, and Masters and Johnson's examination of physiological and anatomical changes reflected attempts to remove the participants' own perspectives. Hite made the voice of the person being studied the very essence of the research. It was therefore no longer the reflecting professional or the researcher who was the sexual expert but both the researcher and the subject of the research. Truths about sex were elicited by an interaction between the researcher and the researched (Figure 3.4).

• What methods are used?	Interviews/essays
• Who is the sample?	A majority
• How are the results presented and analysed?	As an interpretation

Figure 3.4   Methods of the transitional period

Methods of the late twentieth century

In the past two decades of the twentieth century there was an explosion of research into sexual behaviour. Following the identification of the HIV virus in 1982 and concerns about the rising rates of teenage pregnancies and abortions, research focused on the relationship between sex and health and sex and death. It asked questions concerning what sexual practices individuals perform, how they felt about performing them and how they could be helped to perform them in safer ways. Health education interventions were established, the media were activated and funding was made available to establish research teams and promote individual research activity. In the late twentieth century, theories about sex remained essentially biological but the emphasis over the past few years has shifted again from sex for pleasure to sex as risk. The methodologies used to study sex as risk also changed and diversified, ranging from quantitative to qualitative and from atheoretical to theoretical. This section focuses on two groups of recent studies: first, the National Survey of Sexual Behaviour in Britain (Wellings *et al.*, 1994), and second, the Women Risk and AIDS Project carried out in Manchester and London (Holland *et al.*, 1990a, 1990b).

The National Survey of Sexual Behaviour in Britain (Wellings *et al.*, 1994) was a large nationwide survey conceived in the wake of the identification of the HIV virus and an awareness that 'The amount of speculation and discussion of sexual behaviour stands in stark contrast to the lack of reliable empirical evidence' (p. 1). Previous research had examined the sexual behaviour of those individuals believed to be most at risk from HIV such as homosexuals, injecting drug users and prostitutes. In contrast, the authors of the National Survey decided to examine the sexual practices of a representative sample of individuals in Britain. The study was funded by the Wellcome Trust after being originally blocked by the Conservative Party in 1989 as recorded by a headline in the *Sunday Times*, 'Thatcher halts survey on sex'.

What methods did the survey use? Data collection involved preliminary in-depth interviews with a small sample as a means to develop the final questionnaire. This was administered face to face by 488 different interviewers and involved an additional self-completion component which was completed by the interviewee in his or her own time. The authors reported concern for interviewer bias and described how the 'standard quality controls were used' including 'supervision of the interviewers in the field' and 'random check backs on selected interviews' to ensure that interviewers were behaving consistently. They also detailed the methods to assess the reliability and validity of the subjects' answers. This included the careful design of the measures in terms of wording and order of questions, and approaches such as 'reassuring the respondents of the confidentiality of the survey', 'a non judgmental approach in the part of the interviewer', 'the use of neutral questions', 'the avoidance of stigmatising labels', a check at the end of the interview of 'whether they (the respondent) had answered truthfully' and 'a firm understanding on the part of the respondent of the urgent need for the data'. The authors also checked the validity of the subjects' accounts by comparing responses between different parts of the questionnaires and by juxtaposing answers concerning STDs and abortions to other independent data sets.

For sampling, the authors created a reliable sampling frame and selected a random sample of individuals aged between 16 and 59 to result in a sample of about 20,000. The authors identified their sampling frame from the postcode address file, which is a regularly updated computer-held file of largely residential addresses. The authors described this as more reliable than the electoral register but noted that it did not contain information concerning the numbers of individuals living at each residence and excluded the homeless and those living in institutions. Following the identification of the residences to be approached from this sampling frame, the interviewers then randomly selected one person from those eligible using a grid technique. Of those 50,010 addresses selected, 5980 were found to be either businesses, non-residential or unoccupied and 14,228 residents were found to be ineligible, leaving a denominator of 29,802. Of these, a total of 18,876 individuals responded, giving a response rate of 63.3 per cent. The authors described their final sample as a national probability sample which was presented as 'the largest representative sample survey of sexual lifestyles ever undertaken in the British population' (Wellings *et al.*, 1994, p. x). The authors also provided some information on the processes involved in the analysis of the data. They described how the questions asked in the interviews and questionnaires involved boxed alternatives or numbered responses rather than open-ended responses, providing simple numerical data which were subjected to 'clerical editing and a coding stage before the data were keyed into computer'. The data were then checked for missing entries and 'correct routing and for correct code ranges for each variable'. The analyses involved either simple descriptive statistics, or more complex multivariate statistics which are described in the text, largely in the form of footnotes.

Finally, how were the results presented? The most obvious factor concerning the presentation of the results from this study were the absence of comment, interpretation or discussion of any implications. In the main the results were presented in tables with stark descriptions of the answers to specific questions such as 'contraception at first intercourse', 'age at first intercourse', 'marital status and frequency of sex' and 'number of partners'. Each chapter ended with a summary which was restricted to an atheoretical restatement of what had been found. The authors' views were not presented or represented in any way.

In summary, the sexual lifestyles survey collected data using pre-set questions and showed a concern for both researcher bias and the reliability and validity of the accounts given. The authors used a large sample to gather information concerning the behaviours of a representative group of the population. These results were presented uninterpreted by the authors and left for the reader to decipher.

In apparent contrast to the National Survey, a contemporary group of studies was carried out by the Women Risk and AIDS Project (WRAP). This was funded by the ESRC and produced papers published in the early 1990s (e.g. Holland *et al.*, 1990a,b; Thompson and Scott, 1990). The WRAP project used both questionnaires and in-depth interviews, and explored areas such as the role of power in sexual relations, the importance of negotiation in condom use, experiences of sex education and young women's experiences of risk and danger. In terms of sampling, the authors collected questionnaire data from 500 women and interview data from 160 women aged between 16 and 21 in London and Manchester, and in addition used diaries and discussion groups. The authors described their sample as 'purposive rather than random samples' (Holland *et al.*, 1990a) and stated that their aim was to carry out a 'systematic investigation of the sexual practices, beliefs and understanding' (Holland *et al.*, 1990a) of the participants involved who were considered to provide a range of views rather than those which were representative. The authors therefore opted for a heterogeneous sample to provide insights into variation.

For their methods, the authors mainly used quantitative approaches in the form of questionnaires and qualitative approaches in the form of 'intensive interviews'. The questionnaires used simple boxed alternatives with closed questions, whereas the interviews involved an in-depth approach with open-ended questions. However, whereas other researchers using such methods have expressed concern about researcher bias and the need to check the data for reliability and validity (e.g. Kinsey, 1948; Wellings *et al.*, 1994) the authors involved in the WRAP project expressed an allegiance to a very different perspective. First, they were explicit about their own theoretical perspective. For example, when discussing educational interventions they stated that 'it is in this context [AIDS education] that feminist theory research and practice could provide an impetus for change' (Holland *et al.*, 1990a). When considering the use of condoms and the processes of negotiation they argued that 'In feminist social theory sexual intercourse in western societies has been identified not only as a social relationship but also as an unequal relationship in which men exercise power over women' (Holland *et al.*, 1990b). In addition, they were transparent in the aims of their research and, rather than being interested in simple data collection, stated, 'we intend that our findings will feed into public education and debate and will therefore make some contribution to the limitation of HIV infection' (Holland *et al.*, 1990b). They clearly stated that the researcher had a perspective and believed that he or she could not and should not be made a objective tool for data collection.

The emphasis on the researcher's own perspective was also made apparent in the methods used for data analysis. Rather than treating the data as the truth, they stated that 'we are using our analysis of interviews with young women to help problematise the way in which they are held responsible for controlling the spread of AIDS' (Holland *et al.*, 1990a, p. 17). They therefore believed that they were analysing the data as a means to support their views. Likewise, when discussing the gender inequalities in relationships they indicated that 'we have drawn upon our data to illustrate the importance of men's power in sexual encounters and their control of sexual pleasure' (Holland *et al.*, 1990b). Even more explicitly they indicated that the researcher's interpretations are an essential component of the research, particularly when trying to understand how young women attempt to manage risk: 'patriarchal ideology can be identified by the researcher, and sometimes by the informant, but patriarchal power relations remain deeply hidden, masked by love, convention, romance and caring' (Holland *et al.*, 1990a). The researchers' own views are also seen in the ways in which the results are presented and the conclusions that are drawn. For example, they concluded their study of young women's experiences of sex education with the statement,

> Above all from a feminist perspective it [sex education] should empower
> young women to take control of their own bodies to resist abuse and

exploitation, to feel comfortable with and understand the development of their sexuality, to express their sexual desires and have them met in safety.

(Holland *et al.*, 1990a)

The authors of the WRAP project made explicit the role of the researcher's own views rather than attempting to create an objective collector of data. In addition, the authors clearly stated that they were interested in accessing the voices of the women involved in the study rather than using them to support or test any existing hypotheses. For example, they argued that 'these interviews enabled us to explore the ways in which these young women construct and present their biographies, and in particular, their sexual biographies both currently and retrospectively' (Thompson and Scott, 1990). They stated, 'we aim to identify the processes and mechanisms through which young women construct experience and define their sexuality and sexual practice' (Holland *et al.*, 1990a). In summary, the WRAP project involved a study of a large but selected group of individuals. It illustrated a concern for understanding the experiences of those involved in the research and also emphasised the importance of the perspective of the individual carrying out the research.

Research at the end of the twentieth century examined sex within a framework of risk and danger and emphasised the association between sex and health and sex and death. Such work occurred within the context of HIV and fears about the increasing rates of teenage pregnancies and abortions. The focus of this research was coherent. In contrast, the methods appear to be diverse. In terms of the question 'what methods were used?' the National Survey used closed questions, whereas the WRAP study mainly used in-depth interviews. The former emphasised reliability, validity and a concern for objectifying the researcher, while the latter made the researcher's own perspective central to both its data collection and analysis. However, both these methodological approaches indicated an active role for both the researcher and the individual being researched. In the National Survey, the researcher devised the questions. In parallel, the WRAP study researchers interpreted the accounts provided. Likewise, in the National Survey the individuals being researched provided their views and similarly in the latter set of studies the researched provided their experiences. Both parties played an active part in the research process. Although the National Survey used a random sample and WRAP used a purposive one, both aimed to study the masses, to gather information from a range and varied group of individuals and to make generalisations from this information to the population as a whole. Finally, although apparently very different, both studies presented the results in effectively similar ways. The National Survey, with its detached and stark presentation of facts, enabled anyone who read the report to impose their own interpretation and to integrate this with their own

• What methods are used?	Scientific survey/reflexive interviews
• Who is the sample?	Representative majority/ heterogeneous minority
• How are the results presented and analysed?	Without interpretation/ with interpretation

Figure 3.5   Methods of the late twentieth century

experiences. Likewise, the WRAP studies made their own perspective so explicit and transparent that the reader was again left to make up their own mind. Sex research at the end of the twentieth century used everyone as the sexual expert: the researcher, the researched and even the reader of the research (Figure 3.5).

The methodological shifts

The twentieth century saw great changes in its approach to sex from sex for reproduction, to sex for pleasure and finally to sex as risk. The methodologies to produce these theories also changed; from the methods of professional reflection and experience, to the scientific approaches of surveys and laboratories, to the increasing emphasis on the voices of those being researched. There were also shifts in the concerns expressed regarding researcher bias and the validity of the accounts given. The choice of sample also changed from a focus only on the small minority to a study of samples which varied in their degree of representativeness. Therefore, changes have occurred in terms of the methods used to explore sex. If discourse can be said to construct its object, methodology may do the same. In fact, methodology could be said to be the strategy which facilitates this construction. Methodology can itself be seen as a discourse.

Methodology as a strategy for constructing the individual

Research methodologies in the social sciences are developed to describe and understand the individual. They are based upon questions such as 'how do people behave?', 'what do people think?', 'what are the links between what they think and what they do?' and 'what factors relate to both behaviour and thoughts?' They are therefore developed and implemented as a means to describe the self. However, this individual is not the only self being studied. The object of the research (the researched) and the researcher and even the reader of the research are all selves and are all described either explicitly or implicitly by the methodology under question. So how are the methodologies developed to study the individual reflected in the construction of the individual? (Table 3.2). The methodologies used throughout

Table 3.2   The objects of methodology

	Researcher	Researched	Reader
Early twentieth century	Objective	Objective	Objective
Mid-twentieth century	Subjective	Subjective	Objective
Transitional	Interactive	Interactive	Objective
Late twentieth century	Reflexive	Reflexive	Reflexive

the twentieth century consider the issue of bias whether in the form of bias from the person being researched, bias from the researcher or bias from the reader of the research. How this bias is addressed informs the ways in which the individual is constructed through the strategy of methodology.

Early twentieth century

At the beginning of the century, the researchers were the experts who espoused their beliefs about sex based upon their own professional experience and gained authority either from their training, occupation or God. The experts were objective, impassive and unreflexive in their approach. By the very process of relying only upon occasional observations, these impassive individuals were also the minority being studied. The readers of this work were also passive receivers of their insights who lacked any subjectivity. At the beginning of the century bias was not considered and was therefore not addressed. The methodology of the professional experts reflected the three dimensions of an individual who showed an absence of agency and no sense of self.

Mid-twentieth century

By the mid-twentieth century the individual described within sexual research was beginning to change. In parallel with work in the earlier decades the readers of the research remained the passive recipients of knowledge. However, the researchers carrying out the research started to show signs of subjectivity. Although purporting to be the passive collectors of data, their preoccupation with contaminating the data with their own views and their fear of researcher bias suggested a different story. Such precautions were only necessary as the researcher developed a sense of agency, since becoming a subjective self itself created the possibility of bias. In parallel, although adhering to the scientific method in their approach to those involved in the research, the very preoccupation with removing the subjects' personal views illustrated that the subject was becoming able to have such a view. In the mid-twentieth century, therefore, the methodologies developed to study the individual reflected a reader who remained the passive recipient of knowledge. The issue of bias, however, was considered and managed for both the researched and the researcher as they both began implicitly to reveal their subjectivity.

The transitional period

By the late 1970s a further shift in identity can be seen. In parallel with earlier work the reader remained the passive recipient of information. A shift, however, occurred in both the researcher and the researched. In line with the mid-twentieth century, the researcher in this transitional period can be seen to have a personal view and a sense of agency. However, rather than this being revealed through concerns about researcher bias and minimised through the scientific method, this bias became central to the research. Similarly, in line with earlier work the person being researched also had a sense of self. However, rather than being seen as contamination of the data this self likewise became the focus of the works. The Hite Reports illustrated both a researcher and a researched who were no longer implicit but explicit in their subjectivity. However, these two forms of subjectivity were not separate but interacted; the researcher carried out their research via a process of interaction with the researched who in turn revealed their subjectivity via an interaction with the researcher. Methodologies in this period constructed a subjective individual who interacted with other subjective selves.

The late twentieth century

By the late twentieth century the methodologies reflected an alternative version of the individual. The researchers, whether using stark empirical work or in-depth interviews, were subjective either in their development of hypotheses or in their concern for their own ideologies and political agendas. Both the elaborate concern for objectivity shown in the National Survey and the explicit statements of personal perspectives in the WRAP studies are illustrative of a researcher who had a sense of agency. The individual being researched was similarly subjective. For the National Survey the subjects were asked for facts but the concern for recall and response bias, and issues of privacy indicated an individual who had their own personal perspective. This was also illustrated by the WRAP studies' interest in experience, reflections and the voice of the interviewees. Accordingly, in the late twentieth century, bias was an issue for both the researcher and the researched as these individuals became subjective selves. But whereas these two selves had previously interacted with each other, both researcher and researched now worked separately. The research was no longer created in the space between them, as both claimed the right to speak the truth and each functioned independently of the other. Furthermore, the reader also became both subjective and independent. The presentation of the National Survey data left the reader to make up their own mind as to the meaning of the information. No interpretation was given – the reader made sense of the material in their own individual way. Likewise, the WRAP researchers' agendas were made so explicit in the WRAP studies that the reader was permitted to decide first what the data meant and second whether or not they concurred with the researcher's own overt interpretations.

At the end of the twentieth century, bias permeated all aspects of research as all parties became subjective. The researcher changed from professional sexual authority to distant collector of data to becoming increasingly expressive of a personal view. The person being researched shifted from being a passive provider of information, to someone who was increasingly listened to, finally to someone whose voice was no longer an intrusion but the very essence of the research. Finally, even the reader of the sexual literature changed from a passive recipient of sexual knowledge to someone who was expected to interpret and decide for themselves the meaning of the information being presented. But these subjective selves no longer interacted with each other. They became independent beings who were subjective and aware of their subjectivity and interacted with themselves – they had become reflexive.

To conclude

Previous literature has explored the theories around sexual behaviour as a means to assess how different theories construct sexuality. The interviews, questionnaires and laboratory observations used to produce these theories, however, are themselves strategies for constructing the individual. Likewise, the methodological concerns for bias are also constructive strategies. As these strategies change so does the 'nature' of their object; the researcher, the researched and the reader reflecting the three dimensions of the individual. In short, by the end of the twentieth century the methodologies constructed a subjective self who no longer interacted with the outside world or even with other subjective selves but had become a reflexive individual.

Towards a social study of social science . . .

The previous chapter illustrated how a discipline's theories which are used to choose research questions and to frame data can be considered strategies to construct not describe the individual. This chapter has illustrated how this constructive process occurs through the strategies of methodology in terms of data collection and analysis and the sample chosen. In line with this, methodologies over the past one hundred years have increasingly constructed an individual in all its manifestations who is a reflexive self. The transformation of the individual can also be seen through the strategy of measurement. This is the focus of the next chapter.

4 Measurement as data

The example of health status

At the beginning of the twentieth century, health was measured in terms of the absence of death. Towards the end of the century many measures of health emphasised the individuals' own views of their health status. Theories concerning the measurement process have also changed. The process of measurement is conventionally regarded as a means to collect data about the individual. Measurement, however, can also be analysed as a strategy to construct the individual (Table 4.1). To this end, this chapter explores changes in the measurement of health and the accompanying concerns about the measurement process in terms of the questions 'How is health measured?' and 'What theories of measurement have been developed?'

Table 4.1 The roles of measurement

Conventional view	*Alternative view*
Measurement is a tool to collect data about the individual	Measurement is a strategy to construct the individual

Researchers measure a range of variables. Those interested in laboratory science may measure cell replication or decay and the impact of a new drug upon this process. For those interested in clinical medicine, blood pressure, weight or glucose metabolism may form their focus of attention while for the epidemiologists illness prevalence and incidence are important. Such research involves questions such as 'How many cells are there?', 'What is their rate of decay?', 'What is an individual's level of insulin production?' or 'How many new cases of cancer are there each year?' These questions require a simple process of measurement as the cells and cases are counted and the numbers shown on weighing scales or blood pressure machines are recorded. The machines may need to be calibrated but no one asks the questions 'How do you know?', 'Are you sure?' or 'Says who?' What it is, is what is measured, and measurement is simple. For late twentieth-century social scientists the story was different. Although their historical roots lay

Table 4.2   What is measured

Natural science	Social science
cell replication	beliefs
velocity	feelings
blood pressure	social class
glucose levels	values
illness prevalence	ethnicity
temperature	behaviours

in the study of an observable variable, namely behaviour, the increasing emphasis on the complexity of human beings brought with it an interest in beliefs and emotions. Such constructs cannot simply be counted or read from a meter as they are complex and their measurement is a complicated process (Table 4.2). This shift from simplicity to complexity is particularly apparent in the changing approach to measuring health status over the past hundred years.

The changing measurement of health status

Early twentieth-century measurements

Subsequent to the introduction of registration of births and deaths in 1838 the standard measurement of health status was the mortality rate. At its most basic it took the form of a very crude mortality rate which was calculated by simply counting the number of deaths in one year compared to either previous or subsequent years. The question asked was 'Has the number of people who have died this year gone up, down or stayed the same?' An increase in this figure could be seen as a decrease in health status and vice versa. This approach, however, required a denominator as a measure of who was at risk. The next most basic form of mortality rate therefore included a denominator reflecting the size of the population being studied. Such a measure allowed for comparisons to be made between different populations: more people may die in a given year in London when compared to Bournemouth, but London is simply bigger. However, in order to provide any meaningful measure of health status, mortality rates were corrected for age (Bournemouth has an older population and therefore it would be predicted that more people would die each year) and sex (men generally die younger than women and this needs to be taken into account). Mortality rates can also be produced to be either age specific such as infant mortality rates, or illness specific such as cancer death rates. As long as the population being studied was accurately specified, corrected and specific mortality rates provided an easily available and simple measure: death was a good, reliable outcome.

Mid-twentieth-century measurements

Clinical researchers and epidemiologists may accept mortality rates as the preferred measure of health status. However, the incorporation of social scientists into the medical world since the mid-twentieth century has challenged this dichotomous model of health to raise the now seemingly obvious question 'Is health really only the absence of death?' In response to this, from the 1950s there was an increasing focus upon morbidity. However, in line with the emphasis upon simplicity inherent within mortality rates, many morbidity measures still used methods of counting and recording. For example, the expensive and time-consuming production of morbidity prevalence rates involved large surveys of 'caseness' to count how many people within a given population suffered from a particular problem. Likewise, sickness absence rates and caseload assessments involved counting days lost due to illness and the numbers of people who visited their general practitioner or hospital within a given time frame. Such morbidity measures were still relatively simple.

Late twentieth-century measurements

Towards the end of the century, measures of health status increasingly opted for a complex approach to health referred to as measures of subjective health status. For example, self-report measures of subjective health status ranged from single items such as 'How would you rate your own health?' (Idler and Kasl, 1995) to composite scales such as the Nottingham Health Profile (Hunt *et al.*, 1986) and the SF-36 (Ware and Sherbourne, 1992) which ask for individuals' own assessment of their health status. Likewise, quality of life scales in the main focus on individual's own assessment of how their own quality of life has been impaired (e.g. Fallowfield, 1990). In fact, over the past decade, some quality of life scales were developed which asked the subject not only to rate their own assessment of their health status but also to define the dimensions along which it should be rated (McGee *et al.*, 1991; O'Boyle *et al.*, 1992).

A shift in perspective

The shift from an emphasis on mortality to one on quality of life reflects a shift from simplicity to complexity. It also, however, reflects changes along a series of other dimensions (Figure 4.1). First, it represents a shift from implicit value to attempts to make this value explicit. For example, mortality and morbidity measures assumed that what they were measuring was an absolute index of health. The subjects being studied were not asked 'Is it a bad thing that you cannot walk upstairs?' and the relatives were not asked 'Did they want to die?' In contrast, the more complex measures attempted to make the value within the constructs being studied explicit. They asked

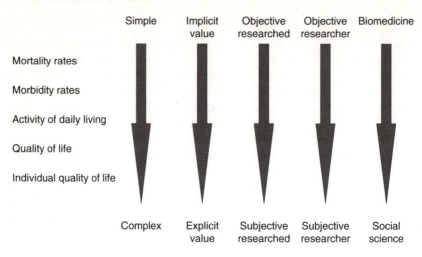

Figure 4.1   A shift in measurement/a shift in perspective

questions such as 'To what extent are you prevented from doing the things you would like to do?' or 'Is your present state of health causing problems with your relationships?' Some measures asked the subjects to describe 'What are the five most important aspects of your life at the moment?'

The second dimension which varies between the simple and complex measures of health is the nature of the individual being studied. Assessments of mortality and morbidity were assumed to be objective scientific measures which accessed a reality which was uncontaminated by response bias. In contrast, the complex measures made this bias the essence of what they were interested in. For example, mortality data were taken from hospital records or death certificates, and morbidity ratings were often made by the health professional, not the individual being studied. In contrast, subjective health measures asked the individual for their own experiences and beliefs. They asked 'How do you rate your health?' or 'How do you feel?' They made no pretence to be objective and, rather than attempting to exclude the individuals' beliefs, they made them their focus. Third, the researcher has also changed from an objective scientist to a subjective individual. For example, mortality and morbidity rates are assumed to be consistent regardless of who collected them. This assumption is problematic, as studies of caseness require definitions of diagnoses, and evaluations of sickness absence rates require a decision to be made about what constitutes being off sick (having a sick note? not taking annual leave?). Choice of data for mortality rates may also be open to bias, and the definition of death may vary across both researchers and time – when does a miscarriage become a still birth which is registered as a death? In contrast, the more complex measures of health found at the end of the century either compensated for researcher bias through the use of self-report questionnaires, closed questions, or in-depth, open-ended interviews to elicit the beliefs of the interviewee. Likewise, some individualised quality of life scales (O'Boyle *et al.*, 1992) presented the subject with a blank sheet and asked them to devise their own scale. Therefore, recent measures of health highlighted that the researcher has a view and attempted to reduce the impact of this on their measurements of health.

Finally, such shifts epitomise the different biomedical and social science perspectives. If health status is regarded as the presence or absence of death, then mortality rates provide a suitable assessment tool. Death is a reliable outcome variable and mortality is appropriately simple. If, however, health status is regarded as more complex than this, more complex measures are needed. Morbidity rates account for a continuum model of health and illness and facilitate the assessment of the more grey areas, and some morbidity measures accept the subjective nature of health. However, it is only measures which ask the individuals themselves to rate their own health which are fully in line with a social science model of what health is. Such subjective measures not only accept but highlight and emphasise health as a complex construct. They provide a measure of health status which is in accordance with the perspective of the discipline. The shift in how health is measured is therefore also reflected in a shift in the very understanding of what health is.

The twentieth century has therefore seen changes in the answer to the question 'How is health measured?' from mortality rates to quality of life scales. This shift in perspective reflects a change from a simple to a complex approach to health status. It reflects a shift from implicit to explicit value and from a biomedical to a social science model of health. It also represents a shift from attempts at objectivity to an emphasis on subjectivity, thereby describing both the individual being researched and the researcher as subjective selves. However, it is not only measures of health that have changed. The twentieth century has also seen changes in the concerns expressed about the measurement process and in the theories of measurement which have been developed to address these concerns.

Concerns about measurement

In the 1920s scientists began to suspect a link between asbestos and inflammation of the lining of the lung and subsequent lung cancer. In the 1940s Fleming noticed that penicillin mould suppressed the growth of bacteria and hypothesised that this might generalise to bacterial diseases in humans. In the 1950s clinicians had a theory that smoking caused lung cancer. To test these theories the researchers needed to confirm links between the different pairs of variables involved. This was uncomplicated with respect to measurement, since asbestos, inflammation of the lung, lung cancer, bacterial growth and even smoking could be evaluated either through observation or in response to simple questioning. No one asked

'How do you know that that is inflammation?', 'Are you sure they smoke?' or 'Have they really been in contact with asbestos?' For early scientific measurements no concerns about the measurement process were expressed.

Over recent years however, the measurement process has raised many concerns for those involved. For example, Blalock in his book *Conceptualisation and Measurement in the Social Sciences* (1982) argued that 'the social sciences are faced with a host of difficulties' and that these problems are 'worthy of our best thinking and immediate and continued attention', with his book's summary stating 'The social sciences are facing serious problems'. According to Blalock, such problems have arisen out of the kinds of research done by contemporary social scientists. Social science researchers theorise that beliefs influence behaviour and that behaviour influences health. They predict that coping style and patterns of adaptation may relate to outcome. In addition, they suggest that social class, ethnic group or social inequality may predict both the onset of and recovery from illness. But how do researchers know they are actually measuring beliefs? Are the measurements of coping accurate? Which measure of social class most closely relates to social class? Before such predictions can be tested they first need to be refined, and the constructs they relate to need to be clarified. Next, an accurate measurement tool for each of the relevant constructs needs to be developed. The two theories of conceptualisation and operationalisation were developed in the late twentieth century as a means to address the concerns raised about the measurement process. Aspects of validity and reliability were developed to faclitate their effectiveness (Figure 4.2).

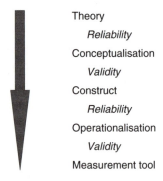

Theory

   Reliability

Conceptualisation

   Validity

Construct

   Reliability

Operationalisation

   Validity

Measurement tool

Figure 4.2   Theory of measurement

Theories of measurement

Stage 1: Conceptualisation

Blalock (1982) defined conceptualisation as 'a series of processes by which theoretical constructs, ideas and concepts are clarified, distinguished and given definitions that make it possible to reach a reasonable degree of consensus and understanding of the theoretical ideas we are trying to express'. Conceptualisation therefore involves the translation of a vague notion into a clearly bounded construct and is essential for any attempts at measurement. It is also essential for communication both within and between academic disciplines, as poorly conceptualised constructs can lead to confusion between research groups and apparently contradictory findings. For example, if a group of researchers were interested in the impact of cervical screening on health, their research conclusions could depend upon how their constructs were conceptualised. If health were conceptualised as 'the detection of abnormal cells', then a biomedical paper may conclude that cervical screening improved health status. In contrast, a psychology paper may conclude the reverse if health were conceptualised as 'anxiety and depression'.

The central role of conceptualisation is particularly apparent in the area of quality of life. Reports of a Medline search for the term 'quality of life' indicate a surge in its use, from 40 citations between 1966 and 1974, to 1907 citations from 1981 to 1985, to 5078 citations from 1986 to 1990 (Albrecht, 1994). Quality of life is obviously in vogue and much research has been done both to develop measures of quality of life and to use these measures in outcome studies. Researchers have differentiated between quality of life in the final year of life (Lawton *et al.*, 1990), quality of life in individuals with specific illnesses (e.g. Meenan *et al.*, 1980), quality of life from a health economics perspective (Rosser and Kind, 1978) or with an emphasis on survival (Bush, 1983). Measures of quality of life have ranged in complexity from single-item scales (Idler and Kasl, 1995) through to multifactorial scales (e.g. Hunt *et al.*, 1986). They have used either a unidimensional approach which focuses on a single aspect of health such as mood (e.g. Goldberg, 1978) or pain (e.g. Melzack, 1975) or a multidimensional perspective which has attempted to encapsulate health in the broadest sense (e.g. Fallowfield, 1990). It has also been defined in a multitude of ways including 'the value assigned to duration of life as modified by the impairments, functional states, perceptions and social opportunities that are influenced by disease, injury, treatment or policy' (Patrick and Ericson, 1993), 'a personal statement of the positivity or negativity of attributes that characterise one's life' (Grant *et al.*, 1990), and more recently by the World Health Organisation as 'a broad ranging concept affected in a complex way by the person's physical health, psychological state, level of independence, social relationships and their relationship to the salient features in their environment' (WHOQOL Group, 1993). However, it remains unclear whether quality of life is different to health status, whether it is the same as subjective health and whether it is separate to health-related quality of life; as a construct quality of life remains poorly conceptualised. In fact, Annas (1990) argued that the use of the term should be stopped altogether. Given that its use continues, how can good conceptualisation be achieved?

Using validity and reliability

Validity refers to 'the issue of how we can be sure that a measure really does reflect the concept to which it is supposed to be referring' (Bryman, 1988). In contrast, reliability 'is concerned with the consistency of a measure' (Bryman, 1988). As a means to assess and promote conceptualisation, social scientists have developed and used aspects of validity and reliability. Face validity is most often described within the context of operationalisation. It is also, however, relevant to the theory of conceptualisation. Face validity requires researchers to believe that a concept makes sense and that its definition reflects the construct itself. Over recent years the WHO has set up a working group to define quality of life (WHOQOL Group, 1993). Similar gatherings were also held to develop the EORTC QLQ-C30 (e.g. Aaronson *et al.*, 1993). Such meetings involve the discussion of which definition makes most sense. In order to be deemed to show satisfactory face validity, the experts must believe that the resulting definition is sensible. Conceptualisation is also facilitated through inter-rater reliability. Again, this term is usually applied to operationalisation. Agreement between experts is, however, implicit to the conceptualisation process as quality of life work tends to be collaborative. Inter-rater reliability is achieved implicitly either through debate and collaboration or via explicit methods such as focus groups and the Delphi method, which involves generating new ideas and commenting on each idea until agreement is reached. A clearly conceptualised construct is therefore one which primarily has face validity. It has to have been defined clearly and can be differentiated from other constructs, and has been generated via inter-rater reliability to show that face validity has been achieved consensually. Therefore, quality of life will have been clearly conceptualised when it is known what it is and what it is not, and conceptualisation will be complete when the experts agree that the chosen definition of quality of life reflects what it really is. The theory of conceptualisation therefore bridges the gap between a vague idea and a focused construct and is facilitated by the use of face validity and inter-rater reliability.

Stage 2: Operationalisation

Once constructs have been conceptualised, the measurement process involves operationalisation which refers to 'the translation of concepts into observable entities' (Bryman, 1988) and reflects the development of an acceptable measure of the construct in question. Lazarfeld (1958) described the 'flow from concepts to empirical indices' in terms of four stages, namely imagery, concept specification, selection of indicators and formation of indices. For constructs such as patient, health professional, child and so on this involves a process not dissimilar to conceptualisation. For example, if a study required the assessment of patient health, the concept 'patient' needs to be operationalised. It could be operationalised in many ways including 'person requiring treatment', 'person registered on a general practice list', or more specifically 'person over the age of 16 attending their general practice in order to see the GP for their own health problem (not accompanying a child or other adult) within a year'. Such constructs therefore simply involve a clear definition and agreement between the researchers involved. Most social scientists, however, are interested in more complex constructs which involve measurement tools such as interviews, semi-structured or structured questionnaires. These constructs also need to be operationalised as a means to develop ways of measuring them effectively. Accordingly, the definition of depression and anxiety is turned into a mood scale and the definition of quality of life can be translated into a quality of life scale. For example, following the discussions concerning an acceptable definition of quality of life the European Organisation for Research on Treatment of Cancer operationalised quality of life in terms of functional status, cancer and treatment specific symptoms, psychological distress, social interaction, financial/economic impact, perceived health status and overall quality of life (Aaronson *et al.*, 1993). In line with this, their measure consisted of items which reflected these different dimensions. Likewise, the researchers who worked on the Rand Corporation health batteries operationalised quality of life in terms of 'physical functioning, social functioning, role limitations due to physical problems, role limitations due to emotional problems, mental health, energy/vitality, pain and general health perception' which formed the basic dimensions of their scale (e.g. Stewart and Ware, 1992). Such tools are usually developed from items elicited from the literature, the researchers, the subjects of the research, or all three. The items are then organised into a questionnaire which is piloted and finalised. The operationalised construct and subsequent scale is assumed to measure the construct under scrutiny. However, the development of a measurement tool raises the question 'Does the tool really measure the construct in question?' How do researchers know that their constructs are being measured by their measurement tools; that the construct has been accurately operationalised?

Using validity and reliability

Aspects of validity and reliability are also used to facilitate accurate operationalisation. To this end social scientists ask a series of questions to ascertain whether the results from the measurement tool are not simply an artefact of the tool itself. First, they ask 'Does the tool produce results which are comparable to those produced by other similar tools?' Construct validity in the form of convergent and discriminant validity deals with the problem of variability by illustrating consistent results when compared to other measures. The next question asked is 'If the construct is conceptualised as being constant can the tool detect this constancy or does it produce different results at different times?' Test-retest reliability deals with the problem of change over time by illustrating that the measurement tool can produce consistent results. Finally, they ask 'Do all items used in the scale reflect different aspects of the same construct?' This problem is dealt with by testing the scale for internal consistency using statistical procedures such as factor analysis and reliability coefficients. By determining a level of agreement between measures, over time and within measures, social scientists create a sense that the tool accurately measures the construct. Operationalisation therefore involves bridging the gap between construct and measurement tool and this process is facilitated by aspects of validity and reliability.

Therefore, in parallel to the shift in the measurement of health status from mortality to subjective health status, there have also been shifts in the concerns expressed about measurement. This has resulted in the development of theories to address these concerns. In particular, late twentieth-century researchers have expressed concerns about accuracy, and have subsequently developed the theories of conceptualisation and operationalisation as a means to bridge the gaps between theory and construct and this construct and the measurement tool. Aspects of validity and reliability have been used to assess and facilitate the effectiveness of the measurement process. When this is done satisfactorily the measurement process is complete, and researchers can be confident that they are measuring the object of their studies. But why do concerns about measurement arise in social science? And why do they arise now?

Why do these concerns arise within social science?

Whether it be biological research examining cell function, epidemiological research examining mortality, psychological research assessing the predictors of smoking or sociological research examining the impact of class on health, there is a biologist, an epidemiologist, a psychologist and a sociologist examining a cell, death certificates, self-reports of smoking or social class. Any research process involves two components: the researcher and the researched. However, early health researchers agreed what cells were, what death was and what changes in cell structure looked like. Likewise, cells were believed to be the same wherever they were and death was considered as death regardless of who had died. Therefore, the constructs of early health research did not need to be conceptualised because there were no dissenting voices. Neither did their constructs need to be operationalised because the object they were measuring was considered the same wherever it was and whoever it belonged to. For early researchers of health there was consensus between researchers and also between whatever was being researched. Concerns about measurement were not raised and the theories of measurement were not needed.

Social science is the study of individuals. The shift in health research towards a social science perspective has increasingly described this individual as having a sense of self and as a subjective being. Therefore, contemporary social science is the study of individuals who vary. Whether it be along the dimensions defined by demographic variables such as age, gender, class, geographical location, or whether it be according to beliefs and behaviours, individuals differ from each other. Social science therefore lacks consensus amongst the researched. However, as social science research is also done by individuals, by default, this shift in perspective has also changed the individuals doing the studying; the researchers have also become subjective. Therefore, social science also lacks consensus amongst the researchers. Concerns about measurement address the issue of consensus. First, the theory of conceptualisation with its use of face validity and inter-rater reliability creates agreement amongst the researchers. Second, the theory of operationalisation and its use of construct validity, test-retest reliability and internal consistency is needed to adjust for variation in the researched. The shift towards an individual who is a subjective found within contemporary health research has therefore problematised both the researched and the researcher. In doing so it has lost the consensus inherent within earlier health research. Theories of measurement with their focus on conceptualisation, operationalisation, reliability and validity bridge the gaps between idea and construct and construct and measurement tool. This is needed to re-establish consensus between both the researchers and the researched (Figure 4.3).

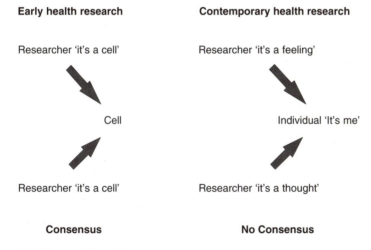

Figure 4.3   The problem of consensus

Bridging or constructing gaps?

Central to empiricism is the belief that the objects of study can be measured and that things 'out there' can be accessed by measurement tools.

Empiricism depends upon the faith that the results produced by these measurement tools are not simply artefacts of the tools themselves. For example, health research is founded upon the assumption that factors such as depression exist in individuals not in depression scales, and that quality of life exists even when it is not being measured. Therefore, if the researcher is regarded as a disembodied being who passively records what is happening in the world, then the gap between themselves and the 'out there' is straightforward; the 'out there' is all there is. Accordingly, theories of measurement involving conceptualisation, operationalisation, reliability and validity are central to the process of bridging this gap between the idea and the construct and ensuring that the assessment results are accurate reflections of things in the world.

At the turn of the twentieth century, however, measures of health emphasised the person being researched as a subjective being. Such measures of health also described the person doing that research as similarly subjective. The researcher is an individual who has a subjectivity comparable to the individuals being studied. Subsequently the gaps between idea, construct and measurement tool become more problematic. Can what is 'out there' ever be measured? Can researchers stand outside their own minds to study someone else's? How can researchers ever know that what they are measuring exists beyond how they measure it? Conceptualisation, operationalisation, reliability and validity are an essential part of the measurement process, but not to create measurement tools which accurately reflect the outside world. These strategies are central to both the creation and perpetuation of the belief that measurement of this world is possible. Accordingly, theories of measurement may not bridge the gaps between idea and construct and between construct and measurement tool. Such theories are strategies for the construction of these gaps. Without the strategies of reliability and validity to authorise the process of conceptualisation, the construct would simply be the creation of the researcher. Without such strategies to give credibility to the process of operationalisation the resulting measurement tool would simply be the construct; nothing else. The researcher would be studying what was inside his or her own head – it would bear no relation to the outside world. Without such strategies to give authority to the measurement process, researchers would simply be reporting their fictional stories about the world as they saw them.

To conclude

The past one hundred years has seen a change in the measurement of health from the use of mortality rates to a focus on subjective health status. This has reflected a shift from implicit to explicit value, from simple to complex measures and from a biomedical model of health to a social science one. In addition, it has illustrated a shift towards both the individual being researched and the individual doing the research becoming subjective beings.

The late twentieth century also saw an increase in concerns about the problems with measurement and the development of theories of measurement as their solution. In particular, theories of conceptualisation, operationalisation, reliability and validity have been offered as ways to ensure that the measurement process is an accurate one. Such theories are conventionally regarded as bridging the gaps between theory, construct and measurement tool. Social science, however, studies individuals who are deemed to be subjective. By default, such individuals are studied by researchers who are deemed to be equally subjective. How can it be known, therefore, that the construct is not simply in the mind of the researcher? How can it be clear that the measurement tool is not simply the construct itself? Perhaps, rather than bridging the gaps between idea and construct and tool, the theories of conceptualisation and operationalisation, reliability and validity give credibility to the belief that the world can be measured. Accordingly, they have been developed as strategies to construct these gaps. Without them researchers would not know that the object of research, the individual, was 'out there'. Without them there would only be a scientific faith that measurement was possible.

Towards a social study of social science . . .

In the same way that a scientific fact is constructed through the practices of science, the social science fact is similarly constructed through the practices of social science. In particular, the strategies of theory, methodology and measurement construct the individual in terms of what it is, an increasingly reflexive and intra-active self in all its manifestations who is detached from their social world. But an object is defined not only in terms of what it is but also in terms of what it is not. The next two chapters explore the use of boundaries to construct what the individual is not.

5 The rhetorical challenge to biomedicine

Latour (1987) called rhetoric a 'fascinating albeit despised discipline' and described the rhetoric of his 'technoscience' in terms of scientific jargon, complex figures and diagrams. The rhetoric of psychosocial disciplines takes an alternative form. Psychologists mystify their work in increasingly complex flowcharts, impenetrable data sets and an incessant search for measurable mechanisms. In contrast, sociologists resort to an interminable referencing of texts, theories and 'great men'. A discipline's textbook is a useful and essential source of rhetoric which reflects the contemporary state of that discipline. Textbooks can be neither revisionist nor revolutionary as they both describe and construct the breadth and limitations of the field. Therefore, an examination of textbooks can provide insights into the consensual nature and aims of the discipline. Accordingly, textbooks in health psychology and medical sociology can be used to reveal the implicit aims and assumptions of the respective disciplines and it is the rhetorical claims of these disciplines and their relationship to the individual which form the focus of this chapter.

The rhetoric of health psychology and medical sociology

Introductory chapters in health psychology textbooks state: 'The biomedical model is facing a serious challenge' (Sheridan and Radmacher, 1992, p. 4), 'An alternative to the medical model is clearly needed' (Kaplan *et al.*, 1993, p. 8), and 'Does the biomedical model need improvement? Yes. Lets see why' (Sarafino, 1990, p. 10). Such proclamations suggest that the discipline of health psychology aims to challenge the biomedical model of health and illness. Even texts aimed specifically at medical students emphasise 'limitations to classical medicine' (Kaptein *et al.*, 2000) and how aspects of health psychology 'provide a clear example of the limitations of adopting a narrow biological approach to health and illness' (Weinman, 1982). In parallel, statements from medical sociology textbooks indicate a similar adversarial alignment between the discipline and biomedicine. For example, Stacey (1988) described a range of 'challenges [that] have been presented to biomedicine from within and without' (p. 174) and more specifically, Nettleton (1995) stated, 'The sociology of health and illness has

Table 5.1 The challenge to biomedicine

Health psychology	Medical sociology
'The biomedical model is facing a serious challenge'	'Challenges have been presented to biomedicine from within and without'

sought to offer alternative ways of interpreting medicine . . . through criticisms of the biomedical model' (p. 4) which is followed by a section called 'Challenges to biomedicine' (p. 5). Similarly, Armstrong, in the introduction to his textbook (1994), stated that 'The arguments in the rest of the book, which attempt to identify some deficiencies of the biomedical model . . . is [*sic*] an attempt to redress the balance' (p. 2). In short, the stated aims of both health psychology and medical sociology indicate that these disciplines present themselves in conflict with biomedicine (Table 5.1). Specifically, they challenge biomedicine's model of the causes of health and illness, of a dualistic individual and of the definition of outcomes and provide their own psychosocial explanations.

Psychosocial causes of health and illness

Biomedical theory and research examine etiology in terms of factors such as viruses, bacteria and carcinogens. Both health psychology and medical sociology question this perspective, the former arguing that psychological factors contribute to the causes of illness, and the latter emphasising the role of social factors: 'Health status is clearly the consequence of factors other than biological . . . [which are] related to social structures and vary according to gender, social class, "race" and age' (Nettleton, 1995, p. 6). For example, research in health psychology has examined the role of stressors in illness causation, and theories of stress argue that appraising a potential stressor as stressful may contribute to a deterioration in health (Lazarus and Folkman, 1987). It has also been suggested that stress may result in changes in health-related behaviours such as smoking, alcohol intake, diet and exercise which play a causal role in ill health (e.g. Krantz *et al.*, 1981). Similarly, medical sociologists have emphasised the role of life events in illness etiology. For example, research indicates that life events which are appraised as stressful may contribute to psychological problems such as depression, chronic illnesses such as coronary heart disease and acute problems such as appendicitis (e.g. Brown and Harris, 1978, 1989). The work of McKeown (1979) illustrated a similar emphasis on psychosocial causality. However, whereas health psychologists highlight McKeown's argument that illnesses in the late twentieth century are predominantly caused by behaviour, medical sociologists focus on McKeown's emphasis on the role of social environment in the elimination of past illnesses. A parallel argument can be seen within the social support literature. For example, the frequently cited longitudinal study by Berkman and Syme

(1979) outlines the causal role of social support in mortality and is central to both health psychology and medical sociology. However, whereas health psychologists emphasise social support as a perception, medical sociologists locate support in the environment. Such theoretical developments away from a biomedical model of causality are encapsulated in Engel's bio-psychosocial model which proposes that health and illness are the result of a complex interplay of a multitude of psychosocial factors (1977). Within this framework, health psychology emphasises the 'bio/psycho' components and medical sociology focuses on 'bio/social' factors. In summary, these theoretical frameworks and the emphasis on beliefs, behaviours and environmental factors propose an alternative way of thinking about the biomedical models' approach to the causes of illness.

An integrated individual

The second arm of the challenge to biomedicine relates to its model of the individual. With its separation of diseases of the mind and diseases of the body and its corresponding speciality divisions, biomedicine describes an individual who is dualistic. Health psychology, however, argues for an integration of the mind and the body, sometimes referred to as an holistic or whole person approach and challenges Cartesian dualism: 'We learn in health psychology that the mind and the body are thoroughly intertwined' (Sarafino, 1990, p. 17). A central example of this perspective is the analysis of pain as a perception and an asserted progression from a biomedical division between organic ('real') and psychogenic ('all in the mind') pain. Specifically, the Gate Control Theory (Melzack and Wall, 1965, 1982) argued that pain should be conceptualised as a perception involving an interpretation and appraisal of physical stimuli. Therefore, proponents of this theory argue for an integration of mind and body and a departure from earlier models which described the individual as divided. A similar integration is suggested within contemporary models of stress such as the transactional theory (e.g. Lazarus, 1975; Lazarus and Folkman, 1987) which proposed that stress was the result of the interpretation, appraisal and adaptation to physical stressors. In parallel to theories of pain, the mind and body are integrated to create the experience of stress. Likewise, models of illness onset which emphasise behaviours such as smoking, exercise and screening similarly advance a disintegration of the mind/body boundary.

Research in medical sociology also emphasises the increasing permeability of boundaries. For example, studies have illustrated the role of social class in predicting coronary heart disease and diet (Marmot and Theorell, 1988) and changes in health and illness during economic recession (Brenner, 1977; Eyer, 1977). Factors such as gender and ethnicity have also been examined in terms of differences in illness threshold (Nathanson, 1977) and their relationship to the allocation of resources and material factors (e.g. Arber *et al.*, 1985; Donovan, 1984). Such research emphasises the location of the individual within a social context and attempts to bridge the social/body divide of biomedicine. In short, research within both health psychology and medical sociology presents itself as a challenge to the biomedical models' conceptualisation of a divided self and asserts an integrated individual.

Non-medical outcomes

The final challenge to biomedicine relates to the choice of outcomes. Biomedicine defines outcomes in terms of medically derived factors such as longevity, disease-free intervals and death. In contrast, health psychology emphasises the role of behaviour. For example, Kaplan, in his paper 'Behavior as the central outcome in health care' (1990), has argued that we should challenge the biomedically defined outcomes such as morbidity and mortality and replace them with a focus on behaviour. He suggests that 'Recognising that health outcomes are behavioural directs intervention towards whatever method produces the most health benefit at the lowest cost' (p. 1211). Both health psychology and medical sociology also focus on the patient's own personal assessments of health status using self-report questionnaires such as the Nottingham Health Profile (NHP) (Hunt *et al.*, 1986) and the SF-36 (Ware *et al.*, 1986) which were developed as a departure from a more objective notion of health. For example, the NHP consists of items relating to pain, physical mobility, sleep, energy, social isolation and emotional reactions. The SF-36 asks similar questions and includes additional items on factors such as social functioning and general health. Likewise, quality of life measures have also been developed which measure subjective health in terms of an integration of functional ability and psychological well-being (e.g. Fallowfield, 1990). Research has also increasingly examined the consequences of health-related interventions in terms of patient satisfaction and compliance (e.g. Ley, 1988). Such measures are used within both health psychology and medical sociology and emphasise outcome in terms of the individual's own self-assessment and represent a departure from a medical perspective.

In summary, health psychology and medical sociology emphasise their adversarial alignment with the biomedical model in terms of the causes of illness, an integrated individual and the definition of outcomes. Theoretical developments within these disciplines support this challenge and promote an emphasis on psychosocial etiology, a disintegration of self-boundaries and patient-defined outcomes. However, are these developments really a challenge? Are these psychosocial approaches really different to biomedicine?

A failure to challenge

Behaviours, beliefs and stressors are presented as alternatives to medical causes, but they are described as facilitating medical causes, the real precipitants. Smoking as a behaviour does not cause lung cancer, it simply provides a medium for exposing the individual to carcinogens. The experience of stress results in fatty deposits and beliefs about safe sex may effect the chances of being exposed to the HIV virus. Although the rhetoric of health psychology indicates a challenge to biomedical causes of illness, examination of the explanatory frameworks suggests an implicit acceptance of this perspective. A psychological approach to etiology is not a substitute for medical causes of health and illness. In fact, health psychology texts at times clearly disparage non-medical causes. For example, on considering cross-cultural differences in lay beliefs about the causes of health and illness, Sarafino (1990) states: 'Recall our discussion of the widespread beliefs in the middle ages about the causes of illness. Today educated people in technological societies generally reject such ideas. But less sophisticated people do not.' He then continues to describe an account of one such person who states: 'I've heard of people with snakes in their body, how they got there I don't know'. Sarafino analysed this account by arguing: 'Although this account was given by a disadvantaged person in the United States it is typical of the level of knowledge generally found in people in underdeveloped countries' (1990, p. 25). Likewise the discipline's analysis of treatment and intervention rejects non-medical explanations of the mechanisms involved. In the context of a cross-cultural analysis of pain management, Gatchel *et al.* (1989) focused on acupuncture and explained that it 'originated in ancient China some two thousand years ago' and that the Chinese explain its effect as a result of 'Chi'i [which] flowed through these meridians' (p. 256). This alternative explanation is juxtaposed to the 'correct' explanation: it 'probably achieves its effects by causing the release of endogenous opiate like substances' (p. 257). As a discipline, health psychology aims to prioritise psychological causes and to acknowledge the role of individual beliefs. However, it implicitly accepts biomedicine's fundamental predicate – its model of etiology.

A parallel pattern can be seen within medical sociology, although with more subtlety than within health psychology. Class, gender and ethnicity are argued to be an alternative set of causes. However, they are not presented as causing illness but as creating a proximity between the individual and the medical causes. Social factors are no substitutes for the real culprits. For example, when considering cross-cultural models of health, Fitzpatrick (1982) argued that 'When a Zande becomes ill or has an accident he may ascribe his misfortune to witch craft . . . These sound strange ways of explaining illness, but the fact is that for the Azande they work. . . . Thus the logic is explained and in any specific episode always "makes sense"' (p. 12). Such an analysis is careful to respect non-medical explanatory frameworks but implicitly rejects them as incorrect. Psychosocial theories of etiology are not incompatible with biomedical ones.

The challenge to biomedical dualism shows a similar pattern. The Gate Control Theory of pain only points towards an interaction of mind and body, not an integration of these components of the individual. Likewise, the transactional theory of stress examines how perceptions may impact on the body, but the mind and body are defined as separate entities which interact: they are not one. The mind/body boundary remains intact. In its call for a disintegration of this boundary, health psychology contextualises the need for an holistic individual alongside philosophers such as Plato and Descartes who are seen as the enemy to be challenged, and Aquinas and St Paul who are cited to reflect the golden age of holistic medicine (Hippocrates appears to have had an ambiguous relationship with the mind/body problem as he is frequently cited as belonging to both camps). This retrospective construction of a time of both dualism and holism provides health psychology theorists both with an object to be challenged and a faith that this challenge is possible. In addition, this construction creates a separation between the discipline of health psychology and the problem of mind/body dualism. The mind/body divide, however, may not be reflection of a biomedical perspective to be challenged by health psychology but a problem created by the very existence of these two disciplinary frameworks. Foucault (1973) argued that modern medicine was developed at the beginning of the nineteenth century and constructed a physical body which was analysed, examined and described. Prior to this time, accounts of the body would have been unrecognisable to the modern biomedical eye. Accordingly, modern medicine described its new objective as supplanting previous and different models of the body. The end of the nineteenth century saw the emergence of the discipline of psychology. In parallel with the previous studies of the body, psychological discourses analysed, examined and described the mind. However, the mind was not developed in order to supersede the body but was described to supplement it. Therefore, the discipline of psychology described its object, the mind, as separate and distinct from the object of medicine, the body. In effect, psychology itself developed the mind/body divide – the problem it is aiming to solve; the existence of psychology as a discipline constructs the very mind/body boundary that it is ostensibly aiming to disintegrate: the juxtaposition of psychology and biomedicine maintains the interaction and nonintegration of the mind and the body.

A similar pattern can be seen for the social/body divide. Medical sociology argues that 'The main determinants of inequalities in health are, however, generally viewed as lying in the material circumstances, lifestyles and behaviours of social classes which produce differences in exposure and resistance to disease' (Morgan *et al.*, 1985, p. 217). The social and the body may interact but remain separated. In parallel to health psychology, sociology, which first emerged at the end of the nineteenth century, located its individual within the social world and medical sociology located its individual within the medical world. Accordingly, the discipline of medical sociology constructs and maintains the social/body boundary it purports to challenge. Therefore, both the disciplines of health psychology and medical sociology can be seen as implicitly biomedical, since they construct their object of study as divided according to biomedical dualisms.

Finally, are the psychosocial outcomes of dysfunction, quality of life and subjective health status different to medically defined morbidity? Are patient compliance and satisfaction a departure from a focus on the value of medical information and medical authority? And are behaviour changes such as smoking cessation and dietary improvement distinct from medical mediators of longevity? In the same way that 'psychology' and 'sociology' constitute a divided individual by defining their object as non-medical, 'health' and 'medical' can only define their outcome as being biomedical.

Privileging biomedical discourses

The inadequate departure from biomedicine's definitions of causality, the implicit construction of biomedical boundaries and the acceptance of medical outcomes represents a failure to challenge biomedicine. It also, however, illustrates a privileging of biomedical discourses. In discussions of cross-cultural models of health and illness, there is a privileging of a medical perspective – Western medicine is correct, other models are interesting but misinformed. In parallel, models of causality prioritise the role of physical input, and psychological and social factors contribute but are simply facilitative and secondary to medical causes. Likewise, the mind and the social world interact and mediate the body, but the body provides the fundamental object to be mediated. An illustration of this privileging process can be found by an examination of the opening chapter headings to most health psychology textbooks, with titles such as 'Physiological bases of behaviour and health' (Gatchel *et al.*, 1989), 'The body's physical systems' (Sarafino, 1990), 'The psychobiological mechanisms of health and disease' (Sheridan and Radmacher, 1992), illustrated throughout with diagrams of the respiratory, digestive, cardiovascular and nervous systems. Similarly, medical sociology texts show a comparable pattern. Stacey (1988) argued: 'it is important to acknowledge the biological base . . . [which] is common to all human beings' (pp. 2, 3) and that there are 'varied interpretations of the biological base' (p. 3), suggesting that biological phenomena exist to be made sense of. In a recent series of books examining the experience of illness ('experience' focusing on individual meaning, and 'illness' differentiating itself from the underlying disease), each book commenced with chapters termed 'Understanding Multiple Sclerosis' (Robinson, 1988), 'Diabetes Mellitus, its nature and prevalence' (Kelleher, 1988), and 'Medical aspects' (Humphrey, 1989), which described the physical processes for each problem. The physical body is presented as the essential hardware to be moderated by the optional psychosocial software.

In summary, health psychology and medical sociology confront biomedicine in terms of causality, but implicitly endorse medical causes. They challenge a dualistic individual, but are intrinsic to the mechanisms creating the divides. Although attempting to offer alternative outcomes, the outcomes being measured are inherently also medical. Not only do they fail to challenge the dominance of the biomedical model but they also privilege the physical body – the backbone of biomedicine. The rhetoric of health psychology and medical sociology describes a challenge to the biomedical model. An analysis of the research literature of these disciplines suggests that this challenge is unsuccessful. Why is there this discrepancy? If psychosocial theories fail to challenge biomedicine, why the rhetoric to the contrary?

Why the rhetoric?

Latour (1987) described rhetoric as a discipline which has 'studied how people are made to believe and behave and [has] taught people how to persuade others' (p. 30). He also argued that the rhetoric may serve either the 'implicit' and 'explicit' interests of those who use it (Latour, 1987). So whose interests does the rhetoric of psychosocial disciplines serve? First, it may serve the interests of individuals such as authors and publishers, who, by suggesting that their approach is original and different, grab their readers' attention. Such controversy may contribute to personal reputations, careers and book sales (Woolgar, 1981). Second, the rhetoric may serve the interests of the psychosocial disciplines via the acquisition of power. Central to medical sociology is the study of the 'dominant' medical profession, and the question 'how a profession succeeded in claiming the right to an exclusive monopoly of health care in the advanced industrial societies' (Hart, 1985, p. 18). Likewise aspects of health psychology have become politicised, and focus on issues of justice and equity and the power of medicine. By 'taking on' biomedicine, perhaps the psychosocial disciplines gain access to the medical world of employment and funding, define a role for themselves in the development of health care policy and acquire some of the power of medicine. The rhetoric may also serve the interests of the psychosocial disciplines in terms of accruing scientific credibility. Latour (1987) described a 'black box' as a theory or 'fact' which is accepted and states that 'no matter how controversial their history, how complex their inner workings, how large the commercial or academic networks that hold them in place, only their input and output count' (p. 3). A black box is a given truth. He argued that black boxes are closed by gathering support and by 'the number of associations [which are] necessary to drive readers out and force them into accepting a claim as a fact' (p. 62). He suggested that these associations can be accrued by the use of rhetoric which becomes more intense as the controversy associated with facts in question increases. He also stated that a similar process is necessary if a black box is ever opened. In line with this, the rhetorical statements of psychosocial texts can be seen as a threat to the black box of biomedicine; they illustrate an assault on the box and serve the interests of the psychosocial disciplines by giving credibility to this assault.

```
┌─────────────────────────────────────────┐
│                                           │
│        The rhetoric as functional         │
│                                           │
│     • For authors                         │
│     • For publishers                      │
│     • For psychosocial disciplines        │
│     • For biomedicine                     │
│     • For disciplinary boundaries         │
│                                           │
└─────────────────────────────────────────┘
```

Figure 5.1   Why the rhetoric?

Third, and in direct opposition to the above explanation, the psychosocial rhetoric may paradoxically serve the interests of biomedicine. Far from confronting their adversary, psychosocial theories of etiology, the individual and outcomes may maintain and perpetuate it. The failure to challenge biomedicine may support and promote it. Kuhn (1962) argued that shifts between paradigms occur when the weight of unexplained anomalies – outliers to the dominant theoretical perspective – becomes too great for the paradigm to bear. Health psychology and medical sociology provide biomedicine with a theoretical explanation for its anomalies, so preventing a paradigm shift. Furthermore, by offering alternative explanations for 'causality', 'individuality' and 'outcomes', psychosocial approaches to health endorse these fundamental parameters of biomedicine. The psychosocial rhetoric of a challenge serves the needs of the biomedical model and the professionals working within it (Armstrong, 1987) (Figure 5.1). Finally, from this functional perspective the rhetoric may serve the interests of both the psychosocial and biomedical disciplines through the formation and substantiation of disciplinary boundaries. The distribution of books in libraries and bookshops reinforces and reflects disciplinary boundaries by defining what belongs and does not belong to a particular discipline. Likewise education is organised along the lines of disciplines and academic careers, and professional titles similarly reflect these disciplinary boundaries. In line with this, the rhetoric of psychosocial textbooks creates and re-creates the boundaries of the psychosocial disciplines. The process of stating what medical sociology is not, simultaneously constructs what it is. In parallel, by stating what health psychology is not, it is also constructed in terms of what it is. By challenging biomedicine, medical sociology and health psychology both state what they are not and therefore what they are. The rhetoric creates the boundary between the disciplines, reinforcing disciplinary discreteness, and the disciplines of medical sociology and health psychology become distinctly non-biomedical.

In short, a discrepancy exists between the stated aims of health psychology and medical sociology and their explanatory frameworks; the rhetoric is not reflected in the underlying substantive literature. Accordingly the disciplines do not live up to their rhetoric and the rhetoric can be analysed as serving the needs of interested parties. Within this analysis, rhetoric has its conventional meaning of overblown claims which may promote reputations, careers or sales and which reflects a battle for power and scientific credibility between disciplines. However, is rhetoric simply functional?

An additional framework

Latour also provided an additional framework for understanding rhetoric. He argued that we should not differentiate between 'the "rhetorical aspects" of technical literature' and other aspects such as 'reason, logic and technical details' (1987, p. 61) but that 'we must eventually come to call scientific the rhetoric able to mobilise on one spot more resources than older ones' (1987, p. 61). Accordingly the rhetoric of science and the science itself are seen as one. Both the overblown claims and the technical details presented to support these claims can be analysed as rhetoric. Likewise, in terms of the disciplines of health psychology and medical sociology, the rhetoric is both the stated aims and the explanatory frameworks; it is both the challenge to medicine and the theories and research which complement it. Within this analysis, the rhetoric not only serves to close and open the black box, the rhetoric *is* the black box. All scientific text can be seen as rhetorical. Likewise so can psychosocial text; the rhetoric is all there is.

If rhetoric is all there is, then rhetoric can be read as a discourse to describe the fabrication of the object of that discourse. In line with the discourses of theory, methodology and measurement, both the rhetoric in the conventional sense (the stated challenge to medicine) and the rhetoric in the unconventional sense (the explanatory frameworks) can be understood as a means by which the object of this rhetoric (the individual) is constructed. The rhetoric is the discourse through which the truth about the individual can be known and it is the discourse through which the individual is constructed. Accordingly, the rhetorical boundary between disciplines created through the stated challenge to biomedicine finds reflection in the boundaries of the body. And by knowing what this self is not, then simultaneously the self emerges as what it is; by being defined as not biomedical the individual inevitably becomes constructed as psychosocial. The rhetorical claims of health psychology and medical sociology of a challenge to biomedicine are reflected in disciplinary boundaries and disciplines which are not biomedical. They are also reflected in the construction of an individual which is, by definition, psychosocial.

A contradictory relationship

The rhetoric of psychosocial texts, however, both challenges and complements biomedicine; it both opposes and supports it. If rhetoric is all there is, then the rhetoric of psychosocial science illustrates a contradictory

---

The rhetoric

A stated challenge	The explanatory frameworks
'Biomedicine is wrong'	*'Biomedicine is right'*
The individual is not biomedical	Biomedicine provides the necessary contrast
The individual is psychosocial	

Figure 5.2   The rhetoric is all there is

relationship within biomedicine. This tension also finds reflection in the construction of the self, for although the individual is constructed as psychosocial, biomedicine is the necessary contrast which facilitates this construction. Biomedicine is both the foe and the reluctant friend, both the enemy and the essential ally. Without biomedicine to endow power upon the individuals working within psychosocial disciplines, without biomedicine to lend these disciplines its scientific credibility and without the juxtosposition of biomedicine to psychosocial disciplines, psychology and sociology would not have a disciplinary identity in their own right. Such power, credibility and disciplinary discreteness is similarly essential for the construction of the psychosocial self. For such an individual needs a potential medical self to describe what it is not in order to know what it is. It needs the contrast of a medical individual to become delineated as a psychosocial one. The rhetorical challenge to biomedicine delineates what the individual is not, while the rhetorical supports for medicine maintain and perpetuate this necessary opposite (Figure 5.2).

To conclude

Textbooks provide a productive insight into the contemporary state of a discipline. This present chapter has explored the textbooks of health psychology and medical sociology, and suggests evidence for a gap between the stated challenge to biomedicine and the implicit acceptance and even privileging of a biomedical perspective. The rhetoric to challenge the dominance of biomedicine is not reflected in the substantive literatures of these psychosocial disciplines. This chapter has explored possible explanations for this discrepancy. First, it has been suggested that rhetoric may be analysed as overblown claims which serve the needs of interested parties – the authors, the publishers, and the respective disciplines by perpetuating disciplinary discreteness through the construction of disciplinary boundaries. The statement of what health psychology and medical sociology are not is reflected in the boundaries delineating what they are.

However, rather than the rhetoric serving a simple function, perhaps the rhetoric is all there is. The rhetoric is both the stated aims and antithetically the explanatory frameworks, both the overblown claims and, in contrast, the substantive literatures. This inherently contradictory rhetoric may be analysed as a discourse and, as with the discourses of theory, methodology and measurement, rhetoric may be read as a means to explore the construction of the object of this discourse: the individual. Therefore, if medical sociology and health psychology are defined through what they are not, then the individual they study is similarly constructed. By being defined as not biomedical, the individual becomes psychosocial. The contradictory relationship with biomedicine is likewise reflected in the boundaries of the individual. Biomedicine may be considered the foe through which the psychosocial self may be compared and therefore defined, but the medical self is simultaneously necessary for such a comparison. Further, the medical individual is simultaneously essential for delineating and maintaining the boundaries of the psychosocial self.

Towards a social study of social science . . .

Theory, methodology and measurement may be read as strategies to construct the individual in terms of what it is. Specifically, over the past one hundred years they have constructed a self who is increasingly intra-active and reflexive. This chapter has explored the role of rhetoric in constructing the individual in terms of what it is not. In particular, the rhetoric of health psychology and medical sociology construct the individual as inherently not biomedical and therefore as psychosocial. A boundary between social science and biomedicine is not, however, the only rhetorical boundary to be found within social science. The boundary between psychology and sociology and its impact upon the individual is the focus of the next chapter.

6 Defining the individual/social boundary

Early psychological and sociological theorists were clear that their disciplines were distinct and that the individual and the social world should be analysed as separate entities. Over recent years, however, the subdisciplines of health psychology and medical sociology have called for an integration of the individual with their social world. To this end, health psychology has drawn upon three theoretical perspectives: social psychology, social epidemiology and social constructionism. In parallel, medical sociology has turned to the use of qualitative methods. This chapter explores the contributions of these perspectives to expanding both the individualistic and social models of health and examines the extent to which the integration of the individual and the social has been achieved. In particular, this chapter examines the changing nature of the boundary between the individual, as represented within psychology, and the social, as reflected within sociology, and explores the impact of such changes on the individual being studied.

The individual and the social in early psychology and sociology

Psychology has its roots in the works of theorists such as Freud, Pavlov and more recently Skinner, who each described an individual who was bounded from their social world. Freud, with his emphasis on the unconscious, the role of repression and the value of symbolism, argued that the influences of social factors such as parenting, economic position and culture were relevant only in their operation via the super ego. For example, when discussing the role of culture Freud argued that

> the past, the tradition of the race and of the people, lives on in the ideologies of the super ego and yields only slowly to the influences of the present and to new changes; and so long as it operates through the super ego, it plays a powerful part in human life, independent of economic conditions.

> (1933, p. 99)

He explicitly described his views on the relationship between psychology and sociology and stated that 'sociology too, dealing as it does with the behaviour of people in society, cannot be anything but applied psychology. Strictly speaking there are only two sciences: psychology, pure and applied and natural science' (1933, p. 216). Pavlov and Skinner likewise indicated both an implicit and explicit separation of the individual from the social world. The use of animals including dogs, rats and pigeons illustrated a focus on the individual concerned rather than their interaction with others, and even these animals were not studied within their natural habitats (even though this was becoming the approach of the contemporary ethologists). Accordingly, early psychology drew upon such approaches and either focused on the workings of the psyche which was seen to subsume the importance of any input from the social world, or on behaviour which was understood in terms of the mechanics of action. From this perspective the individual was regarded as the most fruitful object of study.

Early sociology likewise offered an analysis which differentiated between an individualised and a social perspective. However, in contrast to the work of early psychologists, those influencing early sociology emphasised the importance of poverty, class and economic systems (e.g. Marx, 1849) or directly addressed the relationship between the individual and the social (e.g. Durkheim, 1938). This focus on the social is typified by Durkheim, who argued that 'collective representations, emotions and tendencies are caused not by certain states of the consciousnesses of individuals but by the conditions in which the social group in its totality is placed' (1938, p. 106). His criticisms of psychology with its individualistic perspective were at times more explicit: 'In a word there is between psychology and sociology the same break in continuity as between biology and physicochemical sciences. Consequently, every time that a social phenomenon is directly explained by a psychological phenomenon, we may be sure that the explanation is false' (1938, p. 104). Early sociology saw the individual as subservient to their social world and believed that the social world was of most value for their studies.

In short, early psychology and sociology defined their objects of study as separate and distinct from each other. Over recent years however, there have been shifts within both these disciplines which can particularly be seen within the subdisciplines of health psychology and medical sociology (Table 6.1).

A call for integrating the individual with their social world

Health psychology examines the role of psychological factors in the etiology, prevention and treatment of ill health. In particular it focuses on the role of health-related behaviours such as sex, diet, drug taking and exercise in determining or promoting illness and emphasises the behavioural pathways in moderating stress and pain (e.g. Ogden, 2000; Sarafino, 1990). Recently, the theoretical framework implicit within health psychology has been criticised for its emphasis on the individual and its neglect of the social

Table 6.1   The individual and the social

	Psychology	*Sociology*
The early days	'Sociology too, dealing as it does with the behaviour of people in society cannot be anything but applied psychology' (Freud, 1933)	'Every time that a social phenomenon is directly explained by a psychological phenomenon we may be sure that the explanation is false' (Durkheim, 1938)
Late twentieth century	'Putting health psychology into its cultural sociopolitical and community context is a major priority' (Marks, 1996)	'We need models of the dynamic interactions between organic and psychological process at the level of the individual' (Benton, 1991)

context. For example, Carroll *et al.* (1993) stated that 'Health psychology could be well served by expanding its focus to embrace the study of socio economic health variations, given their magnitude and persistence'. Marks (1996) argued that 'Putting health psychology into its cultural, socio political and community context is a major priority for future development', and 'The assumption that the behaviour of health professionals is determined by their cognitions and nothing more is untenable'. Likewise, Radley (1994) proposed that 'People's experience of health and illness involves both their social context and their body' (p. 17). In addition, in a paper entitled 'Reconnecting the individual and the social in health psychology', Eiser (1996) argued for a need to transcend traditional 'social' versus 'individualistic' theories of health and presented 'the possibility of more general unifying principles' (p. 606). This call for an integration of the individual with their social context also forms the core aim of a recent body of work referred to as 'critical health psychology' (e.g. Crossley, 2000; Murray and Chamberlain, 1999). Thus, recent work within health psychology has explored the individual/social boundary and emphasised the location of the individual within their social world.

In parallel, medical sociology research illustrates a similar emphasis on the problems with the individual/social divide. In contrast to health psychology, medical sociology has traditionally highlighted the social world as its focus for theory and research. For example, the accent on gender, social class, ethnicity, culture and social inequalities has created a central role for the social in its theoretical framework (e.g. Arber, 1991, 1997; Armstrong, 1994; Morgan *et al.*, 1985). However, recent papers have called for a shift away from the emphasis of the social world and a need to address the individual. For example, Figlio drew upon his expertise in psychoanalysis in an essay entitled 'The lost subject of medical sociology' (Figlio, 1987) and suggested that 'medical sociology has lost a crucial dimension from its thinking and methodologies and that this loss – of the subjective dimension

– leaves it vulnerable to medical hegemony' (p. 77). He also argued that 'recent psychoanalysis offers medical sociology an enriched view of the social, one which includes the individual and the social in one field' (p. 95), and suggested that 'subjectivity distinguishes a sociological approach to health and illness from an epidemiological one' (Figlio, 1987, p. 77). The potential integration of the individual with their social world can also be seen within the increasing number of sociological texts focusing on experience, feelings and emotions. For example, the editors of *Health and the Sociology of Emotions* (James and Gabe, 1996) argued that the benefit of connecting sociology with the study of emotions is 'the issue of subjectivities . . . and connecting health and emotions highlights relations not merely between individual and society, but also between person, body and society' (p. 20). Likewise, Williams and Bendelow (1996) followed their argument that the emotions are the missing link between the mind and body with an implicit call to integrate the individual with the social: 'the body is in the mind, society is in the body and the body is in society' (p. 46). They also cited Benton, who stated that sociology needed 'sophisticated models of the dynamic interactions between organic and psychological processes at the level of the individual person and between persons and their social relational and bio physical environments' (Benton, 1991, p. 6). Therefore, although at the beginning of the twentieth century both psychology and sociology analysed the individual and social as separate entities, recent works within these disciplines have called for a dissolution of the individual/social boundary. For psychologists this has expressed itself in a call to study social factors. For sociologists this is reflected in a call to study the subjective individual. To this end health psychology has drawn upon three perspectives: social psychology, social epidemiology and social constructionism. In parallel, medical sociology has increasingly turned to the use of qualitative methods (Figure 6.1).

Psychology	**Sociology**
• Social epidemiology	• Qualitative methods
• Social psychology	
• Social constructionism	

Figure 6.1　Tools to integrate the individual and the social

Developing an expanded health psychology

Using social psychology

Social psychology emerged in the 1950s and established itself as the branch of psychology locating the individual within their social context. This is typified by Tajfel and Fraser (1978) who defined social psychology as 'a discipline which aims at an integration of the psychological functioning of individuals with the social settings, small and large in which this functioning takes place' (p. 17). This shift in emphasis is sometimes attributed to the atrocities of the Second World War and questions such as 'Were the Nazis inherently evil or was their behaviour a product of their culture and history?' and 'Given the right set of circumstance could anyone behave this abominably?' (Brown, 1986). From this time social psychology examined the impact of the social environment upon individual behaviour. For example, research exploring social influence examined phenomena such as conformity, group polarisation, group think and the difference between private and public views (e.g. Asch, 1948; Milgram, 1961, 1974; Moscovici, 1972). Social psychologists also adapted the learning theories of writers such as Pavlov (1927), Wagner (1969) and Rescorla (1967) to develop social learning theories with their emphasis on modelling, observational learning and associative and operant conditioning (e.g. Bandura, 1970, 1977a,b; Bandura and Walters, 1963). Social psychologists developed theories of social interaction and studied interpersonal perception, communication and prejudice (e.g. Argyle, 1967, 1969). Such research emphasised the degree to which individual thoughts and behaviours were dependent upon the thoughts and behaviours of those around them. The discipline of health psychology has drawn upon social psychology in its attempt to develop a less individualistic approach to health and illness. For example, Bandura's social cognition theory (1977b, 1989) has been widely used by researchers attempting to predict and potentially change health-related behaviours including smoking, diet, screening and exercise (e.g. Brubaker and Wickersham, 1990; Norman and Smith, 1995). This theory is based upon the premise that cognitions are shared by individuals living within the same community. In line with this, later social cognition models such as the theory of reasoned action and the theory of planned behaviour (Fishbein, 1967; Ajzen, 1985) included measures of normative beliefs designed to assess directly the impact of important others' beliefs upon the individual concerned. Social psychology has also been drawn upon to explain stress as an interaction between the individual and their environment (e.g. Lazarus and Folkman, 1987), to examine the role of coping and social support as forms of social interaction in the contexts of stress and illness (e.g. Berkman and Syme, 1979; Taylor, 1983) and to explore doctor–patient communication as a form of interpersonal perception (e.g. McNeil *et al.*, 1982). Therefore, social psychology has been used by health psychology as a means to locate the individual within their social context and to dissolve the individual/social divide.

Using social epidemiology

Social epidemiology has traditionally been the domain of both public health medicine and sociology with their focus on health variations. For example, research has explored the extent to which health differentials can be explained by socioeconomic status (Davey Smith *et al.*, 1990; Macintyre, 1986), gender (e.g. Arber, 1997; Bartley *et al.*, 1992), working status (Arber, 1991), income status (Davey Smith, 1996) and ethnicity (Williams and Collins, 1995). Over recent years health psychology has looked to social epidemiology for inspiration on how to include the social context in its assessments of the individual. This has taken several different forms. First, the most simple version has involved the inclusion of demographic variables in psychological models. For example, the health belief model (Becker and Rosenstock, 1984) includes an assessment of the participants' profile characteristics, stress research has explored the role of a woman's working status on illness levels (Haynes *et al.*, 1980), models of coping include a role for demographic and social factors (Moos and Schaefer, 1984), and most researchers collect data on their participants' sex, age, class and ethnic group as a matter of course. Second, a more complex approach to using social epidemiology can be seen in the work of those individuals who have attempted to develop an overarching theory which encompasses both psychological and social phenomena. For example, Marks (1996) used an adapted version of a model devised by Whitehead (1995) as a means to explore the potential integration of demographic factors (including age, sex and hereditary factors), individual lifestyle factors, social and community networks and general socioeconomic cultural and environmental conditions. He argued that behaviour should be understood within its 'ecological context' (Marks *et al.*, 1998, p. 153) and that any interventions designed to change behaviour 'need to be considered in the light of the prevailing environmental conditions which contain the contextual cues for health related behaviours' (Marks *et al.*, 1998, p. 153). In a similar vein, Marmot's model (e.g. Marmot, 1999; Brunner and Marmot, 1999) which integrated both psychological and social factors has been adopted by psychologists as a means to analyse psychological variables alongside social ones (Carroll *et al.*, 1996). A third approach to using social epidemiology has involved analysing how psychological variables themselves may explain and account for health variations. Much of this work has been inspired by the reports of Wilkinson (1989, 1990, 1992) who indicated that it may not only be income differentials between individuals which account for health variations but the overall distribution of income within countries. These data suggested that living in an inequitable society may be bad for health, regardless of an individual's own standard of living. This generated hypotheses as to the possible psychological mechanisms behind this phenomenon (e.g. Carroll *et al.*, 1996). For example, Wilkinson (1992) argued that 'the social consequences of people's differing circumstances in terms of stress, self esteem and social relations may now be one of the most important influences on health' (p. 168). Likewise, Lynch and Kaplan (1997) suggested that 'inequitable income distribution may have direct consequences on people's perceptions of the social environment that influence their health' (p. 306). They argued that 'income inequalities directly influence[s] health through individual appraisals of relative position in the social order' (Lynch and Kaplan, 1997, p. 307). In parallel, Carroll *et al.* (1993) highlighted social relations, psychological stress, uplifts and control as possible psychological mediators. To date, however, little empirical research has supported these hypotheses. In short, health psychology has drawn upon social epidemiology as a means to explore the individual/social divide and locate the individual within their social context.

Using social constructionism

The third approach adopted by health psychology is social constructionism. The origin of this perspective is most often attributed to Berger and Luckmann (1967) who argued that there are essentially two components to social constructionism. First, they emphasised the world as being socially constructed through the social practices of people. Second, they suggested that people make sense of their world and experience this world as pre-given. In the main, health psychologists have adopted the second component of social constructionism and have used it as a framework to examine how individuals construct their social world using a range of qualitative methodologies such as interviews and focus groups. The data generated have then been analysed using methods such as discourse analysis (e.g. Potter and Wetherell, 1987), ethnomethodology (e.g. Garfinkel, 1967), interpretive phenomenological analysis (e.g. Smith, 1996), grounded theory (Glaser and Straus, 1967) and materialist discursive approaches (e.g. Yardley, 1997). This approach has been applied to the study of a range of health-related issues including condom use (Flowers *et al.*, 1997; Willig, 1995), coping (Yardley and Beech, 1998), the adjustment to chronic illness (Radley, 1993), the experience of cancer treatment (Schou and Hewison, 1998) and the experience of being HIV positive (Crossley, 1998). The meanings revealed by the analysis have been conceptualised as both personal and social accounts; thus attempting to integrate the individual with their social world.

Developing an expanded sociology

In contrast to the criticised individualistic approaches of health psychology, over recent years the opposite criticism has been made of medical sociology; namely that it has neglected the individual and that when included, the individual has been considered a subsidiary of the social. Research within medical sociology has therefore attempted to address the issue of the individual by the use of qualitative methods. In line with health psychology, this has involved methods such as interviews and focus groups, and the data derived from these methodologies have been similarly analysed with an emphasis on the themes and categories emerging from the transcripts. However, rather than locating their qualitative methods within the context of social constructionism, medical sociologists have tended to describe their work within the framework of lay beliefs. Specifically, they have used qualitative interviews to examine the meanings attributed to factors such as benzodiazepine medication (North *et al.*, 1995), the doctor–patient relationship (Wiles and Higgins, 1996), stroke (Pound *et al.*, 1998), women's health (Charles and Walters, 1998), cancer (Charles *et al.*, 1998) and general experiences of health and illness (Calnan, 1987). The move towards an emphasis on lay beliefs is also reflected in a burgeoning of texts describing the theory and practice of qualitative approaches (e.g. Creswell, 1998; Dey, 1993; Morse, 1994; Silverman, 1993, 2000). Such studies have explored the individual's experiences, accounts and meanings as an attempt to put subjectivity back into the social world of medical sociology.

Health psychology, therefore, with its traditionally individualistic perspective, has drawn upon social psychology, social epidemiology and social constructionism as a means to integrate the individual with their social world. In contrast, medical sociology, with its traditional emphasis on the social world, has turned to the use of qualitative methods to address the issue of the subjective individual. Accordingly, both these subdisciplines of psychology and sociology have illustrated an attempt to dissolve the individual/social divide. To what extent have they been successful?

Integrating the individual and the social divide

Although social psychology, social epidemiology and social constructionism address the issue of the social world, and qualitative methods address the role of the subjective individual, all these approaches both explicitly and implicitly maintain the separation between the individual and the social. The processes that perpetuate the individual/social boundary can be conceptualised as definitional, methodological and interpretational. Primarily, the boundary is reinforced by exclusive definitions; the individual is defined as non-social, and the social context, in contrast, is defined as non-individual. The methodologies used to explore the individual and the social world operationalise these constructs as being different and then measure them with an exclusive focus on either the individual or the social. Finally, the interpretation of any resulting data also locates the data as belonging either to the individual or the social world. Even when this interpretation attempts to locate the data within both the individual and the social, it is placed as an interaction between the two; an interaction which requires two separate but proximal factors to exist.

For example, for social psychology, the individual's cognitions may be conceptualised as social cognitions and questionnaires are designed at times to assess the cognitions not only of the individual but also of their important others, but they are still operationalised as being located within the mind of the individual being studied. This is epitomised by the following statement given as an explanation of the methods of analysis employed by those using social cognition models: 'This approach is based upon explicit rules guiding individual categorisation on the basis of responses to data collection questions' (Abraham and Sheeran, 1993). The individual may have cognitions about their social world, or resulting from their social world, but these cognitions are still located within the consciousness of the individual. Accordingly, social cognitions are accessed by asking individuals, analysed at the level of the individual and reported to highlight individual differences. Likewise, in a paper attempting to integrate the individual with the social through the use of connectionism, Eiser (1996) suggested that a unified connected system of both the individual and the social could be used. However, within this new model such a unified system appeared to consist of one metaphorical social system and one hardwired individual system – consequently being inevitably un-unified.

For social epidemiology, a similar pattern can be seen. The use of demographics may relate to an individual's social positioning, but to be positioned as an individual within a social world does not indicate that these two elements are merged. In fact, many contemporary measures of demographics specifically ask the subject for their perceived class (e.g. Reid, 1989; Vanneman and Cannon, 1987) or ethnicity (e.g. the UK Census Survey, 1991) highlighting social position as an individualised experience. Complex models which include both psychological and social components still describe these factors as separate and discrete. Likewise, psychological explanations of social inequities are still conceptualised as being 'about' the outside world not inherent to it; for example, as argued by Carroll *et al.* (1993), 'the continuous nature of socio economic gradients invite a search for mediating processes of a psychological nature'. Such mediating processes illustrate a separation of the two elements under consideration, not a blurring.

Finally, in terms of social constructionism and the use of qualitative methods, do these approaches dissolve the individual/social boundary? For psychological research the emphasis has been on an individual's meanings attributed to, explanations about and experiences of the world. As exemplified by Stainton Rogers (1991), this approach examines 'people as clever weavers of stories . . . they can and do create order out of chaos and moment to moment make sense of their world amid the cacophony'. As explained by Radley (1994), 'experiences are significant because they involve people's bodies and their relationship to society'. The social world remains outside the self and the data collected from interviews or focus groups facilitate an exploration of the individual's attempts at making sense of this world. For sociological research, a similar pattern can be seen. Although sociologists have their roots in the study of the social world, by turning to qualitative methods they access an individual's meanings attached to this social world. But they cannot merge these two elements. In fact, the social world appears to be lost. In the same way that social constructionism can only tell the psychologist how an individual constructs their social world, qualitative methods for a sociologist can only do the same. The individual may interact with their social world but again the individual and social world are kept distinct.

Disciplinary discreteness

In short, attempts to integrate the individual and the social are limited by definitional, methodological and interpretational processes. They are also undermined by disciplinary discreteness. The individual has traditionally been the focus of psychology, and the very existence of psychology as a discipline is reliant upon the consistency of this object. From the time of Freud onwards psychology has been defined as the study of the individual in terms of theory, methods and measurement, and without this object of study psychology would disintegrate. The opposite can be said of sociology. At the beginning of the century Durkheim defined the discipline of sociology as the study of the social, and was clear in his differentiations between sociology and the study of the individual. If the individual/social boundary were to dissolve the essence of both these disciplines would be challenged and the disciplines themselves would be under threat of dissolution. Therefore, it is not only definitional, methodological and interpretational processes which maintain and perpetuate the boundary but the very existence of the disciplines supported and protected by this boundary.

So why call for its dissolution? Earlier in this book the psychosocial challenge to biomedicine was understood as primarily functional and as serving the vested interests of the authors, the publishers and the disciplines themselves. This approach is in line with writers such as Latour (1987) and Woolgar (1981) who have focused on the interests of scientists. The claim to merge the individual/social divide also serves the needs of the disciplines for, whilst apparently an attempt to make the boundary dissolve, this claim results in its appearance. If there were no defined difference between the individual and the social, would we know that this difference existed? Likewise if there were no call for its absolution, would we know that it had not been absolved? The call to remove the individual/social divide perpetuates and creates the very boundary it purports to dissolve. The call to challenge biomedicine reifies the differences between psychosocial approaches and those of the biomedical model. Similarly, the call to merge the social with the individual serves the disciplinary function of perpetuating both the divide between the individual and the social and subsequently the differentiation of psychosocial sciences into psychology and sociology.

So why the call now?

The call to merge the individual with the social may function to maintain and perpetuate both the conceptual boundary between these constructs and the disciplinary boundary between the two disciplines. But why has this call

Psychology   Sociology

Before

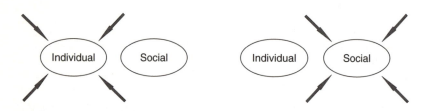

'We need to integrate the individual with the social'

After

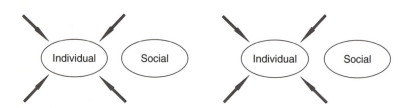

Figure 6.2   The shift in emphasis

happened now, and how does it relate to the construction of the individual? Health psychology has turned to social psychology, social epidemiology and social constructionism to integrate the individual with their social context. However, although these perspectives facilitate the conceptualisation of the individual as interacting with their social world, these two components only interact and do not merge. Therefore, health psychology has been left with a focus on an individual who is separate to their social world. This conclusion is in line with the tradition of individualistic psychology. In turn, medical sociology has turned to qualitative methods to add the subjective individual to its traditionally socially focused discipline. However, medical sociology has not merged the individual with their social world and neither has it remained true to its commitment to the social. At the end of the twentieth century, medical sociology has ended up with a scenario similar to health psychology; a focus on an individual who is separate from their social world. Both these disciplines therefore conceptualise their object of study as the individual who is placed within, but still separate from, their social context. The call to dissolve the individual/

social boundary may function to differentiate between the disciplines. As both these disciplines illustrate a focus on a similarly individualistic object, it may be happening now when the disciplines of health psychology and medical sociology are merging.

Towards a social study of social science . . .

It has been argued in the earlier chapters of this book that the strategies of theory, methodology and measurement have been used throughout the twentieth century to construct an individual in terms of what it is: increasingly reflexive, subjective and intra-active. It has also been argued that the rhetorical boundary between psychosocial theories and biomedicine have constructed the individual in terms of what it is not: biomedical. This chapter has suggested that health psychology also constructs its object as not social. This reflexive, subjective and intra-active individual, however, has not only become the object of focus for health psychology but also for medical sociology. As the strategies of the psychosocial disciplines construct their object as intra-active, even medical sociology, with its traditional emphasis on the social, shifts its focus to study the very object that its strategies have also constructed: the reflexive, subjective and intra-active self (Figure 6.2). The next chapter examines this new individual and suggests that the proliferation of literature on diet epitomises this new self.

7 Who is this late twentieth-century individual?

The example of diet

Dieting, overeating, anorexia and bulimia nervosa are in vogue. Reports show that everyone is dieting and that the prevalence and incidence of eating disorders are on the increase. Consequently, hospitals are opening specialist centres to accommodate this new clinical problem, and self-help groups and those facilitated by professionals are proliferating. In parallel to these changes, experts have used a range of methodologies and developed measures to assess food intake. In addition, they have developed theories about the causes of the various forms of eating behaviour. Earlier chapters of this book have examined the role of the strategies of theory, methodology, measurement and boundaries in the construction the individual throughout the twentieth century. This chapter asks 'who is the late twentieth-century self?'and argues that the construction of this individual is reflected in the increasing interest in a range of eating-related behaviours; the emphasis on such behaviours increases as eating becomes the ideal vehicle to control this new self-controlling, reflexive and intra-active self.

Changing models of the individual

The theoretical perspectives within a discipline are considered vehicles for developing hypotheses and locating results. The methods used and the measures developed are regarded as practical tools for data collection (Table 7.1). Changes can be seen, however, across theory, methodology and measurement which are reflected in a changing model of the individual. In particular, it has been argued earlier in this book that the psychological theories of health and sociological and medical theories of risk describe a shift in their object from a passive responder, to one who interacts with their world to one who has become increasingly intra-active. It has also been argued that methodological changes and the accompanying development of measures reflect an individual who is increasingly reflexive. This model of the reflexive 'intra-active' individual described by late twentieth-century texts regulates, controls and manages their own self and is epitomised

Table 7.1 The role of a discipline

Conventional view	Alternative view
Methodology, measurement and theory are tools to understand the individual	Methodology, measurement and theory are strategies to construct the individual

by psychological and sociological theories, measures and methodologies relating to eating behaviour.

Psychological theories

Eating behaviour in normal weight individuals

Throughout the 1960s and 1970s psychological theories of eating behaviour emphasised the role of food intake in predicting weight. Both empirical and theoretical research examined the behavioural predictors of overweight and obesity and evaluated the eating behaviour of the obese and the non-obese in order to develop theories of etiology. Schachter's externality hypothesis suggested that although all people were responsive to environmental stimuli such as the sight, taste and smell of food, and that such stimuli might cause overeating, the obese were highly and sometimes uncontrollably responsive to external cues (Schachter, 1968; Schachter and Gross, 1968; Schachter and Rodin, 1974). It was argued that this over-responsiveness was responsible for the development of obesity. In support of this, research examined the eating behaviour and eating style of the obese and non-obese in response to external cues such as time of day, sight, number and salience of food cues and taste. Within this framework, the object of the theories about eating behaviour was an interactive individual who interacted with and appraised cues in the environment.

However, during the late 1970s a new model of eating behaviour emerged from psychological theory. Spitzer and Rodin pointed out that 'of twenty nine studies examining the effects of body weight on amount eaten in laboratory studies . . . only nine reported that overweight subjects ate significantly more than their lean counterparts' (Spitzer and Rodin, 1981) and contended that obesity may not be a product of over-responsiveness to external cues. Hibscher and Herman (1977) suggested that trying to eat less (i.e. restrained eating) was a better predictor of food intake than weight per se. Restraint theory was developed as a means of predicting and evaluating eating behaviour and represented a shift from perceiving weight – a biological construct – as the main determinant of eating behaviour and introduced restrained eating – a psychological construct – as a means to evaluate food intake (Herman and Mack, 1975; Hibscher and Herman, 1977). Restraint theory not only represented a shift in the theoretical perspectives of causes of food intake (from biology to psychology), but also represented a shift in the underlying psychological model of the individual.

• Passive eater	'Food was there'
• Interactive eater	'I smelt the food and wanted it'
• Intra-active eater	'I couldn't control my desire for food'

Figure 7.1   Changing model of the eating individual

Restraint theory analysed food intake as resulting from the individual's self-regulation, self-control, self-efficacy and, in effect, described an individual who no longer interacted with their environment but was intra-active (Figure 7.1).

The intra-active overeater

Herman and Mack (1975) explored overeating in normal weight individuals and, using a laboratory-based paradigm, concluded that whereas non-dieters showed compensatory eating behaviour, dieters consumed more following a high-calorie food. This form of overeating was labelled *disinhibition* and has been shown in response to a range of triggers such as high-calorie foods, foods only believed to be high calorie, low mood, stressful situations and smoking abstinence (Herman and Mack, 1975; Herman and Polivy, 1975, 1989; Ogden, 1992, 1994; Spencer and Fremouw, 1979). Several theories have been developed as a means to explain the phenomenon of disinhibition. For example, Herman and Polivy (1984) developed the boundary model of food intake and claimed that the overeating found in dieters was a response to a transgression of the diet boundary. They suggested that eating a high-calorie food lowered mood and stressors created a breakdown in the dieter's self-control. Within this framework overeating reflected a 'motivational collapse' and indicated a state of giving in to the overpowering drives to eat. Such an emphasis described the individual as self-regulating and controlling and conceptualised overeating as a consequence of a failure of this self-control.

To support this model of overeating Glynn and Ruderman (1986) developed the eating self-efficacy questionnaire as a measure of the tendency to overeat. This model of overeating also placed the emphasis on self-regulation. Ogden and Wardle (1991) analysed the cognitive set of the disinhibited dieter and suggested that such collapse in self-control reflected a passive model of overeating and that the 'what the hell effect' as described by Herman and Polivy (1984) may have contained elements of passivity in terms of factors such as 'giving in', 'resignation' and 'passivity'. The emphasis on the transgression of boundaries, motivational collapse and shifting cognitive states emphasised self-control and suggested that overeating was a consequence of the failure of this self-control.

The emphasis on either the presence or absence of self-control is also found in the use of escape theory to explain disinhibition (Heatherton and Baumeister, 1991). This perspective has been applied to both the overeating characteristic of dieters and the more extreme form of binge eating found in bulimics and describes overeating as a consequence of 'a motivated shift to low levels of self awareness' (Heatherton and Baumeister, 1991). It is argued that individuals prone to overeating show comparisons with 'high standards and demanding ideals' (p. 89) that result in low self-esteem, self-dislike and lowered mood. It is also argued that inhibitions exist at high levels of awareness when the individual is aware of the meanings associated with certain behaviours. In terms of the binge eater or overeater, a state of high self-awareness can become unpleasant, as it results in self-criticism and low mood. However, such a state is accompanied by the existence of inhibitions. The individual is therefore motivated to escape from self-awareness to avoid the accompanying unpleasantness. But although such a shift in self-awareness may provide relief from self-criticism, it results in a reduction in inhibitions thereby causing overeating. Therefore, within this analysis disinhibitory overeating is indicative of a shift from high to low self-awareness.

The application of escape theory was a novel approach to the problem of overeating. However, central to this model remains the concept of self-control. The model characterised the individual's 'natural state' as one of disinhibition and indulgence, akin to a Freudian model of the id, or a biological model of instincts. The individual in this state had no self-control and did not respond to the inhibitions and constraints resulting from norms of acceptable behaviour. The state of high self-awareness, on the other hand, reflected an 'unnatural state' and the success of these norms as the individual possessed self-control. Therefore a shift to lower self-awareness resulted in reduced self-control and the drives to eat being released. Again, the escape theory of overeating emphasised self-monitoring, self-control and described an individual who was intra-active.

Theories of motivational collapse and the failure of inhibitions characterised the individual as passively responding to a breakdown in self-control. An alternative model of overeating in normal weight individuals contended that overeating reflected an active decision to overeat. A series of studies indicated that dieters respond to high-calorie foods with an increase in an active state of mind characterised by cognitions such as 'rebellious', 'challenging' and 'defiant' (Ogden and Greville, 1993; Ogden and Wardle, 1991) and that such a shift in cognitive set resulted in overeating. It was argued that rather than simply passively giving in to an overwhelming desire to eat as suggested by other models, the overeater actively decides to overeat as a form of rebellion against self-imposed food restrictions. This rebellious state of mind was also described in obese binge eaters who report bingeing as 'a way to unleash resentment' (Loro and Orleans, 1981) and was implicit in the notion of 'what the hell' as described by Herman and Polivy (1984).

Eating as a form of rebellion may not only be a response to eating restrictions and food deprivation but may at times also indicate a rebellious statement against the deprivation of other substances such as cigarettes (Ogden, 1994) and against deprivation of emotional support (Bruch, 1974). However, although such a model of overeating reconceptualised the overeater as active rather than passive, central to this re-evaluation of overeating remained the concept of self-control. The individual did not eat as a passive response to the breakdown in self-control but as an active defiance of self-imposed regulations. Self-control and self-regulation were central facets of the model. In short, theories of overeating in those of normal weight described the individual as self-controlling, self-regulating and as intra-active (Figure 7.2).

```
• Overeating
• Eating self-efficacy
• Self-denial
• Bingeing
• Disinhibition
• Motivational collapse
• Self-discipline

. . . self-control
```

Figure 7.2 Psychological theories of the intra-active eater

The eating disorders

In parallel to the above theories of eating by normal weight individuals, theories of eating disorders showed a similar pattern of change in their description of the individual. Throughout the 1960s and 1970s research into anorexia nervosa emphasised the role of cultural norms, social expectations and developmental influences. Such an approach focused on the individual's appraisal of these influences and described the individual as interacting with their outside world. Since the late 1970s, although acknowledging the role of environmental factors, anorexia has been described in terms of self-control. For example, Garfinkel and Garner (1986) suggested that the achievement of ever-decreasing weight becomes a sign of mastery, control and virtue. Crisp (1984) likewise compared the anorexic to the ascetic in terms of his or her 'discipline, frugality, abstinence and stifling of the passions' (p. 210), and analysed anorexia as resulting from a determination to keep 'the impulse to ingest at bay' and as a consequence of a 'never ending vigilance and denial'. Bruch described the anorexic as having an 'aura of special power and super human discipline' (1985). In a similar vein, DSMIII-R presented a diagnostic criterion for anorexia as a 'refusal to maintain normal body weight' indicating individual will and control as central to the diagnosis (APA, 1987).

Bulimia nervosa similarly came to be understood in terms of self-control; but in contrast to anorexia nervosa the absence of this control was emphasised. For example, Cooper and Taylor (1988) stated that 'episodes of excessive uncontrolled eating are a central feature' of bulimia. Bulimia was also described as resulting from 'a profound and distressing loss of control over eating' (Cooper and Fairburn, 1986). Likewise, 'irresistible cravings for food' was a central factor of the diagnostic criteria set by Russell (1979). Binge eating was similarly defined by Fairburn (1984) as 'episodes of eating which are experienced as excessive and beyond the subject's control' (p. 235). In short, contemporary descriptions of both anorexia and bulimia emphasised either the presence or absence of self-control and described an individual who interacted with themselves.

Measures of eating behaviour

Self-control is also central to measures of disordered eating behaviour (Figure 7.3). For example, the Eating Attitudes Test (Garner and Garfinkel, 1979) included items such as 'display self-control around food' and 'have the impulse to vomit after meals', both implicating self-control and regulation as important. A similar model of eating disorders can be seen in the Eating Disorder Examination (Cooper and Fairburn, 1987) which included items such as 'attempting to obey dietary rules which relate to attempts to control body shape, weight or body composition' and 'fear of losing control over eating'. In addition, empirical studies have examined differences in self-control between eating-disordered subjects and controls and have examined control in terms of eating self-efficacy, internal locus of control and perceived and actual control (Shisslak *et al.*, 1990; Wagner *et al.*, 1987; Williams *et al.*, 1990). In summary, anorexia and bulimia have been analysed in terms of the individual's ability to control themselves.

```
• 'Displays self-control around food'
• 'Fear of losing control over eating'
• 'Eating self-efficacy'
• 'Attempts to control body shape'

. . . self-control
```

Figure 7.3   Measurements of the intra-active eater

Methodological shifts

A shift towards a self-controlling intra-active self may also be seen within the changing methods used to assess eating behaviour (Table 7.2). In particular, a shift can be seen in terms of the three parties involved in

Table 7.2   Methodology and the intra-active eater

	Methods	Researcher	Researched	Reader
Early twentieth century	Observation/ Expertise	Objective	Objective	Objective
Mid-twentieth century	Laboratory	Subjective	Subjective	Objective
Late twentieth century	Experimental/ Qualitative	Reflexive	Reflexive	Reflexive

research: the researched, the researcher and the reader of the resulting text. Research on food intake at the beginning of the twentieth century is scarce, with food either being used as a demonstration of social inequalities (e.g. Rowntree, 1901), cultural rules (e.g. Richards, 1932) or as a basic biological drive (e.g. Freud, 1933). The methodologies at this time are often poorly described and rely mainly upon reflection from the experts (e.g. Freud, 1933) or objective observations of interesting tribes (Richards, 1932). All parties involved in such research were characterised as devoid of subjectivity and as passively producing or receiving information. In contrast, the mid-twentieth century saw a burgeoning of research in this field with a concern for obesity and development of diagnostic categories of eating disorders. In the main, such studies used laboratory experiments with subjects being asked to eat food under controlled conditions whilst being exposed to a range of stimuli. For example, human subjects were asked to eat after their perception of time had been manipulated (Schachter and Gross, 1968) or following a state of fear arousal (Schachter, 1968). Likewise in a classic study, a group of conscientious objectors from the Korean War were observed under controlled conditions during a prolonged period of food deprivation (Keys *et al.*, 1950). Such methodologies treated those being researched as 'thoughtful rats' who processed the information in the environment and whose behaviour was conceptualised as a product of this appraisal. The participants in the research were characterised by their subjectivity which was minimised by an application of the scientific method and strategies to address response bias. The researchers, likewise, were considered to be subjective selves but were protected from their own subjectivity via strategies to remove experimenter bias. In contrast, the reader of the resulting texts was considered to absorb any results issued to them. Therefore, by the mid-twentieth century the researcher and researched involved in eating-related studies had transformed from objective and passive providers or recipients of data to subjective individuals. Methodologies used to study eating behaviour, however, showed a further shift towards the end of the century. Although much of this research still used experimental methods, the subject was no longer considered to be responding to external cues to eat but to internal ones. Researchers examined how respondents reacted to their internal drives to eat, their internal moods and their internal cognitive sets (e.g. Herman and Polivy, 1984; Ogden and

Greville, 1993; Ogden and Wardle, 1991). The individual being studied was increasingly considered as an intra-active self. More recently both the researcher and the reader of the texts have emerged as reflexive individuals with the increasing use of qualitative methods to address the meaning assigned to food. This has taken the form of clinical insights into the experience of treating anorexics (e.g. Lawrence, 1984), reflections from ex-sufferers (e.g. Chernin, 1981), semi-autobiographical novels relating the experience of women with eating disorders (Ellmann, 1988; Shute, 1992) and research studies designed to explore women's experiences of dieting (e.g. Ogden, 1992) and the meaning of a range of eating behaviours (e.g. Benveniste *et al.*, 1999). From this perspective, those being studied were viewed as reflexive individuals and it was their reflections and views which were of interest to the researcher. The researcher was also given a sense of self either through the polemic narrative or the explicit use of fiction, and the reader was no longer considered as a passive recipient of information but one who actively reflected and made sense of the given text. Therefore, the methods used to explore eating behaviour have changed, with contemporary approaches highlighting the intra-active late twentieth-century self within all three individuals central to the research process: the researched, the researcher and the reader.

Women's own reports of self-control

This chapter has analysed theoretical, methodological and measurement texts. Such descriptions are developed by 'experts' and gradually transformed into the accepted truths about diet. The way in which non-experts understand diet and eating behaviour may be different; expert accounts may differ from those provided by the lay person. Likewise lay and expert accounts may reveal a different model of the individual. An examination of women's own accounts of their eating behaviour suggests that this is not the case; parallel models of diet may be found in both expert and lay accounts. The interview data from a study of twenty-five women who were attempting to lose weight suggest that the experts' descriptions about diet and its focus on self-control finds reflection in women's own accounts (Ogden, 1992). The results from this study indicated that the women described their dieting behaviour in terms of the impact on their family life, a preoccupation with food and weight and changes in mood. However, the concept of self-control transcended these themes. For example, when describing how she had prepared a meal for her family, one woman said, 'I did not want to give in, but I felt that after preparing a three-course meal for everyone else, the least I could do was enjoy my efforts'. The sense of not giving in suggests an attempt to impose control over her eating. In terms of the preoccupation with food, one woman said 'Why should I deprive myself of nice food?' and another said 'Now that I've eaten that I might as well give in to all the drives to eat'. Such statements again illustrate a sense of self-control and a feeling that eating reflects a breakdown in this control. In terms of mood, one woman said that she was 'depressed that something as simple as eating cannot be controlled'. Likewise this role of self-control was also apparent in the women's negative descriptions of themselves, with one woman saying, 'I'm just totally hopeless and weak, and though I hate being fat I just don't have the willpower to do anything about it'. Contemporary diet-related texts describe eating behaviour in terms of self-control and conceptualise a late twentieth-century individual who is intra-active. In parallel, lay discourses illustrate a similar emphasis on self-control and describe a comparable model of the individual.

In summary, across a number of apparently distinct psychological texts the eating individual of the late twentieth century is constructed as a self-controlling self. This individual is also described as reflexive and intra-active. Sociological theories of eating and food illustrate a similar shift in their model of the individual.

Sociological theories

Early theories of food

Whereas early psychological theories focused on the mechanisms of food intake and described the individual as responding to their environment, the traditional (and minimal) place of food within sociological texts has been as an illustration of social order. For example, early writers such as Engels and Marx regarded food as an essential component of human subsistence and its absence as an illustration of inequality (see Mennell *et al.*, 1992). Accordingly, such an analysis focused on food as being located in the environment and as an illustration of variations due to gender, class, culture or ethnicity. In line with this, Elias (1978) used food as an illustration of the development of table manners and placed his discussion within the context of discrepancies between classes and changes over time. Likewise, Lévi-Strauss analysed cuisine in terms of the reflection and reproduction of differing social structures, and Douglas focused on food as an illustration of rules, boundaries and in particular the delineation between the sacred and profane (e.g. Douglas, 1966; Lévi-Strauss, 1965). Within these early sociological texts the emphasis was on food (not eating) as external to the individual and as a means of illustrating difference. Food was given a symbolic role which has been developed in more recent texts focusing on the meaning of food in religion (e.g. Loveday and Chiba, 1985), family relationships (Murcott, 1983) and social rituals (Piette, 1989). In parallel with early psychological theories of the individual as a passive responder, the individual within this sociological literature was characterised by an absence of agency.

- 'Self-constraints'
- 'Internalised control'
- 'Restraining the problem of overweight'
- 'Personal control'
- 'Pseudo power'

  . . . self-control

Figure 7.4 Sociological theories of the intra-active eater

Theories of self-control

Since the late 1970s, however, there has been an increasing interest in food and eating within sociological theory with writings highlighting a more significant role for the individual. In particular, contemporary theories illustrate an emphasis on an individual who has self-control (Figure 7.4). For example, Mennell argued that changing food preferences and cuisines should be understood in the light of social and political changes, and that the availability of plenty resulted in the need for individuals to impose control upon their food consumption (Mennell, 1985, 1986). He also suggested that whereas to gorge was a sign of wealth in times when access to food differentiated between the classes, the rich now need to illustrate self-control as a means to separate themselves from the lower classes. In particular, he suggested that taste and appetite should be analysed within the 'broader shift in the balance between external constraints and self constraints' and that 'more internalised control became valued more than the brute capacity to stuff' (Mennell, 1985; Mennell *et al.*, 1992). This emphasis on self-control can also be seen in Van Otterloo's analysis of eating and appetite in The Netherlands as she suggested that 'the working class . . . is less successful than the middle class in restraining the problem of overweight' (Mennell *et al.*, 1992; Van Otterloo, 1990). The use of the term 'restraining' suggests that overweight is a response to an internal desire to eat that needs to be controlled. Recent sociological theories on diet and eating have also been developed by Turner (1982, 1992), and his work illustrated this contemporary model of the individual as self-controlling. For example, in his analysis of Cheyne's theory of dietary schema in the 1740s, Turner argued that 'Cheyne's dietary management involved a disciplining of the aristocratic, not the labouring body' (1992, p. 190) and suggested that Cheyne's work could be interpreted as similar to Methodism by 'subordinating the body'. He focused on Cheyne's belief that 'medical practice was seen to be secondary to sensible dieting in servicing this hydraulic apparatus' (1992, p. 184). Accordingly, Turner's analysis of these earlier texts emphasised the importance of self-regulation and self-control. Turner also analysed the work of Bruch and her writings on eating disorders. He suggested that Bruch argued that 'self imposed starvation provides a form of personal control which is expressive of pseudo power' (1992, p. 221) and that 'not eating expresses autonomy from parental demands'. Therefore, Turner's analysis of the discourse of diet emphasised the role of self-control and suggested that in Cheyne's time control was important to resist temptation, and that in the late twentieth century a similar pattern of denial had emerged in the form of dieting and eating disorders. In fact, this shift to an intra-active model of the individual is also illustrated by the changing meaning of the word 'diet'. Early in the century, 'diet' was used predominantly as a noun to reflect the external availability of food. Late in the century it was mainly used as a verb 'to diet', emphasising the individual's ability to control food intake.

The status of text

Sociological texts on diet therefore illustrate a shift in their model of the individual similar to that found in psychological theories, with earlier texts describing an indistinct individual who responded to external factors and more recent works attributing the individual with self-control. However, sociological texts present the problem of the status of texts and the relationship between primary and secondary sources. Whereas psychological texts have explored the mechanisms of food intake by collecting original data, recent sociological writings have analysed other texts. This raises the questions 'Does a late twentieth-century analysis of an eighteenth-century text belong now or then?' and 'Does the individual described within such an analysis reflect a modern model of the individual or a model contemporaneous to the original publication?' An exploration of Turner's analysis of Cheyne's work illustrates this problem (Turner, 1992). Turner argued that Cheyne was interested in the role of self-control and self-regulation. From this perspective, the quotes from the eighteenth century appeared to have described a late twentieth-century self-controlling individual. However, an examination of Cheyne's text suggests that this may be a reflection of Turner's own explanatory framework. For example, Cheyne is quoted as saying 'the inventions of luxury, to force an unnatural appetite' and 'Since our wealth has increas'd . . . The tables of the rich and the great . . . are furnish'd with provisions of Delicacy, Number and Plenty, sufficient to provoke, and even gorge the most large and Voluptuous appetite', and 'the richest foods and the most generous wines, such as can provoke the Appetites, Senses and Passions in the most exquisite and voluptuous manner'. Such quotes are analysed by Turner as reflecting a role for self-control. An alternative analysis indicates that Cheyne regarded eating as a response to the availability of plenty. Cheyne also remarked that the availability of 'fermented and distilled liquors [are the cause of] all or most of the painful and excruciating distempers that afflict Mankind'. His use of terms such as 'provoke', 'force', and his emphasis on the impact of an increasing range and amount of food suggests that eating was regarded as a response to external factors; that the individual had no choice but to eat because such a wealth of food has become available. Cheyne may have described an eating individual who was in line with the passive responder revealed by early psychological and sociological theories. As a late twentieth-century writer, however, Turner analysed this text in terms of self-control. As sociology developed an interest in the body, in its status and regulation and as constructionist models of surveillance have become increasingly recognised (Armstrong, 1995), diet – as a means to control the body – became a suitable area for sociological study. Accordingly, the sociological writings on diet have increased in number, and such works have emphasised the role of self-regulation and self-control in diet both in terms of its contemporary status but also in terms of its historical origins.

In summary

Examination of psychological theories of diet suggests a shift in their model of the individual from a passive responder to external events, to one who interacts with these events to a late twentieth-century individual who is reflexive and intra-active. Examination of sociological theories illustrates a parallel shift which is also reflected in lay theories about eating behaviour. A similar shift in the model of the individual can also be found within the changing measures developed to assess eating behaviour and the move towards increasingly reflexive methodologies. Therefore, the late twentieth-century self is described as reflexive and intra-active. Moreover, the focus on self-control is epitomised by the interest in eating behaviour as diet becomes the vehicle for this control and the anorexic reflects the ultimate self-controlling intra-active individual.

Towards a social study of social science . . .

The social studies of science examines the ways in which scientific facts are produced. This book has explored the ways in which social science facts are produced with a focus on the strategies of theory, methodology, measurement and rhetorical boundaries. In particular, it has argued that these strategies construct the individual as a reflexive, intra-active and self-controlling self who is not biomedical and not social. This chapter has illustrated how this new individual is epitomised by the literature on diet. The final chapter explores the implications of this analysis for the relationship between discourse and its object and for the disciplines of psychology and sociology.

8 Health and the construction of the individual

Concluding remarks

The social studies of science has explored science as a discourse and how science constructs its object: the scientific fact (e.g. Latour, 1987; Mulkay, 1991; Woolgar, 1981;). In line with previous research (e.g. Danziger, 1990; Giddens, 1991; Henriques *et al.*, 1984; Rose, 1985, 1990) this book has explored social science as a discourse and how this discourse constructs its object: the individual. However, rather than examining the construction of the individual through the dissemination of knowledge (Giddens, 1991; Rose, 1985, 1990) or the use of such knowledge within social practices such as racism and organisational assessment (Henriques *et al.*, 1984), this book has addressed how the object of social science is constructed through the mechanics of knowledge production. It has explored how these means of production have changed over the twentieth century and has argued that the discourses of theory, methodology and measurement are strategies which construct the individual in terms of what it is. It has also argued that rhetorical boundaries are strategies which construct the individual in terms of what it is not. What does this exploration reveal about the late twentieth-century self?

The late twentieth-century self

Theory is conventionally considered as the framework within which decisions about data collection, analysis and interpretation are made. If theory itself is analysed, however, then changes in this theory are reflected in a changing individual. In particular, whereas theory at the beginning of the century described an individual who was a passive responder to their world, theory in the mid-twentieth century described one who interacted with their world. In contrast to both these models of the individual, theory at the end of the century describes an individual who interacts with their self: an intra-active individual.

Methodology is implicit within many works of social science; in some it is made explicit but it is almost always regarded as a tool to collect data. These data are then analysed and used to tell a story. Methodologies over the twentieth century, however, also tell a story and illustrate a transformation in the three objects of research, namely the researched, researcher and reader. The person being researched has shifted from passive provider of information to a reflexive self (reflected in the shift from 'subject' (being studied), to 'respondent' (completing information) to 'participant' (actively involved)). The researcher has likewise been transformed from an objective expert who passively collected data to one who is aware and explicit in their ideology and subjectivity. The reader of the resulting texts has also changed from one with no sense of agency to one who increasingly interprets and is aware that they are interpreting the texts. In the late twentieth century, the strategy of methodology constructed an individual in all its manifestations who is increasingly reflexive.

The process of measurement is conventionally also regarded as a tool for data collection. The procedures of operationalisation and conceptualisation and processes of affirming reliability and validity are considered necessary for the collection of accurate data which provide an insight into the world. These processes, however, can also be read to provide a story, and suggest a shift in the individual whose characteristics are being measured. A similar transformation may also be seen in the researcher doing the measuring. Measurement in the late twentieth century can be considered as a strategy which constructs both parties involved in research as increasingly subjective and reflexive. This presents a fundamental challenge to the very essence of measurement – that the researcher can assess what is 'out there'. Therefore, measurement can be read first as a strategy to construct its objects as reflexive selves. Second, it can be seen, not as a process to bridge the gap between researcher and researched, but as a strategy to construct this gap – the very essence of the belief that things can be measured.

An object, however, may be defined in terms of what it is and also what it is not. An analysis of the boundaries established by sociology and psychology highlights what the individual constructed by these disciplines is not. First, the discipline of medical sociology and health psychology claim to challenge biomedicine. Second, over recent years these disciplines purport to integrate the individual with their social world. However, an analysis of these stated aims indicates that they are rhetorical which belies the substantive literatures of these disciplines. Such rhetoric can be conceptualised as a strategy to construct boundaries between biomedicine and the psychosocial approaches to health and between psychology and sociology. The rhetoric can also be considered to construct boundaries between the objects of these disciplines such that the individual studied by these disciplines is constructed as not biomedical and simultaneously as not social.

In short, the object of health-related texts in psychology and sociology has undergone three changes in identity. The individual at the beginning of the century was characterised by their passivity and was described as an objective producer and recipient of information. In contrast, by the mid-twentieth century this individual had become a subjective self who

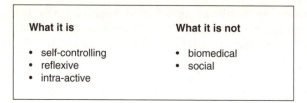

What it is	What it is not
• self-controlling • reflexive • intra-active	• biomedical • social

Figure 8.1   The new individual

appraised and interacted with their environment. By the late twentieth century, the disciplines of psychology and sociology constructed their object not only as subjective but as having an awareness of their subjectivity. This individual no longer interacted with their environment but their focus had turned inward towards themselves. This third identity emerged as a reflexive and intra-active self who was not biomedical and not social and is epitomised by the preoccupation with eating behaviour and eating disorders as diet presents the vehicle for the self-control central to this new individual (Figure 8.1). This new reflexive self is not described by the social science literature or revealed by its studies. It is constructed through the mechanics of knowledge production.

A multitude of selves

Numerous writers have described a multitude of different selves and the ways in which the individual manifests itself. The individual revealed by the present study of psychological and sociological texts on health finds reflection in Giddens' notions of the 'reflexive project', 'high reflexivity' and the 'reflexive self' (1991) and is similar to that described by Stevens (1996c). These selves are aware of their own existence and actively negotiate this self-awareness and reflexivity. They no longer interact with the outside world but have internalised this world and have become intra-active. This self-controlling and intra-active self also reflects the autonomy of the 'distributed self' as described by Bruner (1990), since they can create and re-create themselves as desired. In addition, there are parallels between this individual and the 'autonomous, self contained individual with a rich conscious and even unconscious inner life' described by Smith (1994, p. 406). But rather than being integrated with their social world as described by the 'social self' (Wetherell and Maybin, 1996) this self has become increasingly detached and individualised. Rather than being immersed 'ever more deeply in the social world' as described by Gergen's 'saturated self' (1991) this individual has become insular and self-regulating. And rather than having a 'lack of personal conviction and self worth' as in Cushman's 'empty self' (1990) this individual has self-control, self-efficacy and introspection. Can different versions of the self co-exist? And why are there so many descriptions of the self?

Some research describes a range of selves which are deemed to co-exist and to be accessible by different methodologies and different perspectives. For example, the 'defensive self' (Thomas, 1996) is accessible through a psychoanalytical approach and a 'biological self is accessible through physiological methods (e.g. Toates, 1996). But rather than co-existing or being different versions of the self, these selves are located within a given time and space. Therefore, as argued in this book, a passive self was characteristic of work at the beginning of the century, an interactive self was apparent in the mid-twentieth century and the intra-active reflexive self emerged at the end of the century. In line with this, the multitude of selves described in the literature can be located within their current time and space. They may appear to be contradictory, conflicting and different, but they are perhaps all expressions of the same individual: the late twentieth-century self. Toates, Cushman, Gergen, Rose, Giddens, Stevens and Lasch (and even Ogden) described a different type of self with different charac-teristics and a different relationship to their social world, but they produced their descriptions of this self at the same time. These multitude of selves, while appearing disparate, are expressions of the same self; the reflexive self. The individual was transformed over the past one hundred years and became reflexive at the end of the twentieth century. This transformation involved all the manifestations of the individual including the researcher. And these researchers did what reflexive individuals do, they reflexed and described themselves. The multitude of different selves are all reflexive selves describing what they see when they reflex.

Why have these changes happened? The problem of causality

Recent sociological and psychological health-related texts on theory, methodology and measurement describe a very different individual from the one outlined at the beginning of the century. The nature of disciplinary and conceptual boundaries has also changed. Why have these changes occurred?

Such a change in conceptual perspective would conventionally be under-stood in terms of theoretical progression and accuracy – theories now are a better approximation to the truth than their earlier counterparts. Within such an epistemological framework, change is attributed to increasingly superior methodologies and measurement tools, the accumulation of knowledge and improvements in the use of this knowledge to develop improved theories. But were psychologists at the beginning of the century wrong? Were their contemporary sociologists equally naive? Is it only now that we understand the true nature of our subjects? And indeed, is progress a determinant of change or only a post-hoc explanation?

The shift towards an intra-active and reflexive individual has obvious political undertones; contemporary models of the individual may be a result of a shifting political perspective. The collapse of the Berlin Wall, the increasing popularity of the New Right, a focus on self-help, new concepts of personal responsibility and blame; the new configuration of the individual may be caused by a new emerging political ideology. From this perspective discourses in the late twentieth century would better fit the facts because these facts have been distorted by the economic policies of the dominant political powers. However, politics is only one of the many changing theories. Why select politics as the cause, why not psychology, medicine, epidemiology, sociology? Is this an adequate model of causality? If changes in psychosocial theory are caused by politics, what causes political change?

In the opening chapter to this book it was argued that the potential relationships between discourse and its object can be conceptualised according to the realist, interpretive and constructive models. It was also suggested that these models represented an increasingly problematic relationship between discourse and its object. An alternative way to explore the issue of causality is to examine changes over time within the framework of the discourse/object relationship. It is conventionally believed that the object of social science (the individual) is distinct from social science as a discourse (the discipline). Change to either the discipline or the individual is considered to be driven by outside forces. Such an analysis is in line with both the realist and interpretive models of the relationship between discourse and object with changes to the object driving changes in the discourse. For example, political, environmental or biological factors may change the individual, which results in parallel changes in the discipline. The conventional analysis of change also finds reflection in the supposedly more radical stance of the constructive model. For although the constructive approach represents a shift from privileging the object and illustrates an attempt to problematise the discourse/object relationship it still relies on a linear basis to causality. The object may not cause the discourse, but from a constructive perspective the discourse may be said to determine its object. Causes are still seen as coming from outside the object (the individual) as with the realist and interpretive models, but the driving force is considered to be the discourse. The conventional approach to change has not been challenged. An alternative explanation of change, however, can be understood within a fourth model of the relationship between discourse and its object. From this perspective, recent descriptions within a discipline (the discourse) represent a closer approximation to the true nature of the object of that discipline (the individual), not because the discourse is a product of its object, or because the object is a product of the discourse but because discourse and its object are mutually constitutive. Within this reanalysis, discourse and the object that it 'reveals' become part of the same dynamic and mutually constitutive unit. Discourse and its object become inseparable and the discipline and the individual become as one (Figure 8.2).

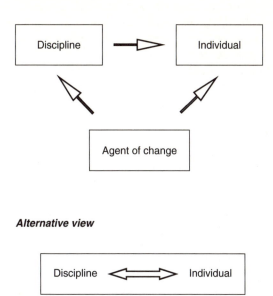

Conventional view

Discipline

Individual

Agent of change

Alternative view

Discipline

Individual

Figure 8.2 The causes of change

How have these changes happened? The problem of methodology

This book is based on the premise that discourses describing theory, methodology, measurement and boundaries can be used as data and that an analysis of these data can enable an exploration of the relationship between discourse and its object: the individual. If discourse can be treated as data, then how are these data to be analysed? What methodology is to be used? Over the twentieth century, methodology can be divided into three dominant approaches, each of which has implications for analysing discourses as data.

The first approach involves collecting data and using these data to develop theories. For example, an inductivist methodologist would observe the data and induce their implications for the development of a suitable theory. Data collection would be seen as being an objective and theory-independent process and the inductivist researcher would be 'outside' the process of data analysis. Therefore, in terms of the data presented within this book, such an analyst would consider psychological and sociological discourses of the twentieth century to speak for themselves; the changing individual identity emerges from the observations provided by the data – an essentially passive process. The changes identified by methodological processes are therefore a product of progress and increasing accuracy. Such a methodological approach finds reflection in the concept of the researched, researcher and reader as passive responders both to each other and to the data and an early model of an individual who passively responds to their environment.

If observations are not objective but theory-dependent, then analysts, like individuals, become subjective. The second methodological approach, therefore, would involve collecting, analysing and interpreting data according to the theoretical perspective of the researcher. In terms of the data presented earlier, this methodological approach would regard psychological and sociological discourses of methodology, measurement, theory and boundaries as research material to be examined. In contrast to a passive approach however, this perspective would emphasise the outcome of this examination as being influenced by the subjective state of the researcher. In line with this, the models of a changing individual are a consequence of the interpretation and subjective analysis of data by the researcher, and data are transformed by the researcher through the use of methodology. This methodological approach describes a researcher who interacts with their data and finds reflection in a mid-twentieth-century model of an individual who interacted with their environment.

If contemporary models of the individual, however, describe an individual who is intra-active, then the researcher is also intra-active. The third methodological approach therefore regards discourse as linked to the object of that discourse (the individual). The researcher and their methodological approach used to explore that discourse are also intrinsic to the discourse; methodology is as part of discourse as are individuals themselves. Not only, therefore, can the discourse and the object be seen as part of a mutually constitutive unit. All manifestations of the individual including the researched, researcher and reader and all aspects of the mechanics of knowledge production including methodology, measurement, theory and boundaries are part of the reflexive and intra-active unit (Figure 8.3).

Therefore, in answer to the question 'How are these changes analysed?', the method of analysis is itself a reflection of the contemporary model of the individual. If this book were written at the beginning of the twentieth century I could claim to be passively responding to the existing data. Psychological and sociological discourses as data would be allowed to speak for themselves and changes in these discourses would be explained as progress. If written in the middle of the century, however, the methodology used to analyse the discourse of social science could be said to accept the theory dependency of these data and the subjectivity of the author. The data would be analysed according to an interaction between the researcher and his or her data and changes in theory would be a product of an interpretation of the data by the researcher. If, however, contemporary discourse does not describe, interpret or construct its object but is mutually constitutive with its object, and if methodology, measurement, theory and boundaries are themselves a facet of this discourse, then discourses as data can only be analysed in the present using methodologies of their time – intra-active methodologies. Equally, this

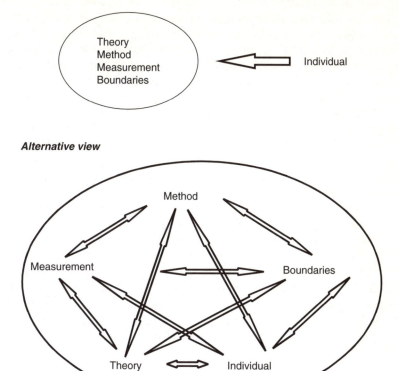

Figure 8.3 Discouses of social science and their object

book, the data it describes and the questions it addresses cannot transcend the theoretical and methodological framework of the late twentieth century. The intra-active individual as described by contemporary psychological and sociological theories finds reflection in the contemporary interest in reflexive methodologies (e.g. Creswell, 1998; Morse, 1994; Silverman, 1993; 2000; Smith *et al.*, 1995; Yardley, 1997). Furthermore, it finds reflection in the ever-burgeoning descriptions of the self which are increasingly the end-point of such methodologies (Gergen, 1991; Giddens, 1991; Bruner, 1990). And the methodology used to analyse changes in the individual can only employ such reflexive approaches to their data.

Health and the construction of the individual

In summary, health-related texts within psychology and sociology illustrate an individual who has transformed through three identities, namely a passive responder, an interactive self and finally a reflexive and intra-active individual. If discourse and its object are seen as part of the same mutually constitutive unit then these changes in individual identity emerge out of changes from within this unit. If this unit is also constituted from all manifestations of the individual and all aspects of the mechanics of knowledge production, then individual identity is fabricated from within such a space. Previous literature has explored how individual identity is constructed through social science discourse. Some of this work has explored how the self is fabricated through the dissemination of social science knowledge. For example, Giddens (1991) drew upon social research to illustrate how self-identity is constructed through the 'reflexive project'. Rose (1985, 1990) argued that centres of power such as the military, therapists, schools, counsellors and businesses shape and construct the ways in which we think about ourselves; 'our private self'. Henriques *et al.* (1984) focused on how psychological knowledge shapes individual subjectivity via its use in social practices such as organisational assessment and racism. The analysis of health-related sociological and psychological texts in this book suggests that individual identity may be constructed through the dissemination of knowledge. But this analysis also illustrates how individual identity emerges out of the mechanics central to knowledge production. The individual is not described by social science literature; it is constructed through the ways in which this literature is used. The individual is also constructed by the strategies employed to generate the knowledge central to its description.

Implications for psychology, sociology and the social studies of science

This study of social science has implications for the disciplines it has considered. In the late twentieth century the object of psychology has been constructed as reflexive. This object has become separate and distinct from its social world and by interacting with itself, it has become self-controlling and intra-active. Such an object is compatible with the aims of contemporary psychology and its individualistic focus and the discipline of psychology thereby remains intact. As Smith argued, 'the cultural focus . . . on the autonomous, self contained individual . . . may be partly responsible for the plurality and proliferation of psychology as a science' (1994, p. 406). The reflexive self can also be seen as responsible for the preoccupation and interest in health as the inner workings of the self become the focus for much of the reflexivity. In parallel, the object of sociology has likewise become a reflexive and intra-active individual. Unlike psychology, however, such a shift represents a digression from this discipline's traditional focus, as the object of sociology has changed from the social to the individual who is characterised by its separation from the environment. At the end of the twentieth century the object of both psychology and sociology has become as one: the intra-active self.

The shift in the model of the individual towards an intra-active self also has wider implications. If the individual being researched has become reflexive and intra-active then researchers have also become increasingly detached from their outside world. If the discourses of social science construct their object as a reflexive and intra-active individual, then can such an individual be a researcher of others? Can psychology and sociology adapt to such a perspective and can these disciplines survive within such a framework? Can research be carried out, data be analysed and papers be written if the researcher involved in such processes is truly intra-active? Does this mean that academic papers cannot be differentiated from novels, research from poetry and social science from fiction? Harré and Gillett argued in 1994 that 'this drift in the theoretical base of psychology threatens to destroy its subject matter entirely . . . the mind lacks any independent reality as a self existent cluster of processes and states . . . the mind is in some sense a social construction' (Harré and Gillett, 1994, p. 22). Likewise Gergen (1991) argued that at the turn of the twentieth century 'the very concept of an authentic self with knowable characteristics recedes from view' (p. 7). If the individual is constructed as intra-active by theoretical, methodological and measurement discourses, then psychology and sociology may study this intra-active individual. But if the researcher is also intra-active then perhaps such study becomes an impossibility. In short, if the triad of the researched, researcher and reader all become intra-active, the boundary between social science and fiction blurs. The social study of social science confounds the relationship between discourse and its object. In doing so it casts doubt on the very essence of the scientific disciplines it studies. It also problematises the disciplines of social science that were its inspiration.

References

Aaronson, N.K., Ahmedzai, S., Bergman, B., Bullinger, M., Cull, A., Duez, N.J., Filiberti, A., Flechtner, H., Fleishman, S.B. and de Haes, J.C. (1993) The European Organisation for research and treatment of cancer QLQ-C30: a quality of life instrument for use in international clinical trials in oncology. *Journal for the National Cancer Institute*, 85, 365–376.

Abraham, C. and Sheeran, P. (1993) In search of a psychology of safer-sex promotion; beyond beliefs and text. *Health Education Research; Theory and Practice*, 8, 245–254.

Ajzen, I. (1985) From intention to actions: a theory of planned behavior. In J. Kuhl and J. Beckman (eds), *Action-control: From cognition to behavior*. Heidelberg: Springer, pp. 11–39.

Albrecht, G.L. (1994) Subjective health status. In C. Jenkinson (ed.), *Measuring Health and Medical Outcomes*. London: UCL Press, pp. 7–26.

American Psychiatric Association (APA) (1987) *Diagnostic and Statistical Manual of Mental Disorders*, revised 3rd edn. Washington, DC: American Psychiatric Association.

Annas, G.J. (1990) Quality of life in the courts: early spring in fantasyland. In J.J. Walter and T.A. Shannon (eds), *Quality of Life: The New Medical Dilemma*. New York: Paulist Press.

Arber, S. (1991) Class, paid employment and family roles: making sense of structural disadvantage, gender and health status. *Social Science and Medicine*, 32, 4, 425–436.

Arber, S. (1997) Comparing inequalities in women's and men's health: Britain in the 1990s. *Social Science and Medicine*, 44, 773–788.

Arber, S., Gilbert, G.N. and Dale, A. (1985) Paid employment and women's health: a benefit or a source of role strain? *Sociology of Health and Illness*, 7, 375–400.

Argyle, M. (1967) *The Psychology of Interpersonal Behaviour*. Harmondsworth: Penguin Books.

Argyle, M. (1969) *Social Interaction*. London: Methuen.

Armstrong, D. (1983) *Political Anatomy of the Body: Medical Knowledge in Britain in the Twentieth Century*. Cambridge: Cambridge University Press.

Armstrong, D. (1986) The invention of infant mortality. *Sociology of Health and Illness*, 8, 211–232.

Armstrong, D. (1987) Theoretical tensions in biopsychosocial medicine. *Social Science and Medicine*, 25, 1213–1218.

Armstrong, D. (1993) Public health spaces and the fabrication of identity', *Sociology*, 27, 3, 393–410.

Armstrong, D. (1994) *Outline of Sociology as Applied to Medicine*. Oxford: Butterworth Heinemann Ltd.

Armstrong, D. (1995) The rise of surveillance medicine. *Sociology Health and Illness*, 17, 393–404.

Armstrong, D. (1998) Decline of the hospital: reconstructing institutional dangers. *Sociology of Health & Illness*, 20, 4,: 445–457.

Armstrong, D. (2002) *The Invention of Identity: Man Through the Prism of Medicine*. London: Palgrave.

Asch, S.E. (1948) The doctrine of suggestion, prestige and imitation in social psychology. *Psychological Review*, 55, 250–276.

Balint, M. (1964) *The Doctor, his Patient and the Illness*. London: Pitman.

Bandura, A. (1970) Modeling therapy. In W.S. Sahakian (ed.), *Psychopathology Today: Experimentation, Theory and Research*. Itasca, IL: Peacock.

Bandura, A. (1977a) *Social Learning Theory*. Englewood Cliffs, NJ: Prentice Hall.

Bandura, A. (1977b) Self efficacy: toward a unifying theory of behaviour change. *Psychological Review*, 84, 191–215.

Bandura, A. (1986) *Social Foundations of Thought and Action: A Social Cognitive Theory*. Englewood Cliffs, NJ; Prentice Hall.

Bandura, A. (1988) Self efficacy conception of anxiety. *Anxiety Research*, 1, 77–98.

Bandura, A. (1989) Human agency in social cognitive theory. *American Psychologist*, 44, 1175–1184.

Bandura, A. (1990) Perceived self efficacy in the exercise of control over AIDS infection. *Medienpsychologie*, 2, 23–43.

Bandura, A. (1991) Self efficacy mechanism in physiological activation and health-promoting behaviour. In J. Madden (ed.), *Neurobiology of Learning, Emotion and Affect*. New York: Raven Press, pp. 229–270.

Bandura, A. and Walters, R.H. (1963) *Social Learning and Personality Development*. New York: Holt, Rinehart & Winston.

Bandura, A., Reese, L. and Adams, N.E. (1982) Micro-analysis of action and fear arousal as a function of differential levels of perceived self efficacy. *Journal of Personality and Social Psychology*, 43, 5–21.

Bandura, A., Ross, D. and Ross, S.A. (1963) Imitation of film mediated aggressive models. *Journal of Abnormal and Social Psychology*, 66, 3–11.

Bandura, A., Cioffi, D., Taylor, C.B. and Brouillard, M.E. (1988) Perceived self efficacy in coping with cognitive stressors and opioid activation. *Journal of Personality and Social Psychology*, 55, 479–488.

Bandura, A., Taylor, C.B., Williams, S.L., Mefford, I.N. and Barchas, J.D. (1985) Catecholamine secretion as a function of perceived coping self efficacy. *Journal of Consulting and Clinical Psychology*, 53, 406–414.

Bartley, M., Popay, J. and Plewis, I. (1992) Domestic conditions, paid employment and women's experience of ill-health. *Sociology of Health & Illness*, 18, 455–475.

Baumeister, R.F. (1986) *Identity: Cultural Change and the Struggle for Self*. New York: Oxford University Press.

Beck, K.H. and Lund, A.K. (1981) The effects of health threat seriousness and personal efficacy upon intentions and behaviour. *Journal of Applied Social Psychology*, 11, 401–415.

Beck, U. (1986) *The Risk Society. Towards a New Modernity*. London: Sage Publications.

Becker, M.H. (ed.) (1974) The health belief model and personal health behavior. *Health Education Monographs*, 2, 324–508.

Becker, M.H. and Avard, J. (1986) Self efficacy, outcome and attrition in a weight reduction program. *Cognitive Therapy and Research*, 10, 319–338.

Becker, M.H. and Rosenstock, I.M. (1984) Compliance with medical advice. In A. Steptoe and A. Mathews (eds), *Health Care and Human Behaviour*. London: Academic Press.

Becker, M.H. and Rosenstock, I.M. (1987) Comparing social learning theory and the health belief model. In W.B. Ward (ed.), *Advances in Health Education and Promotion*. Greenwich, CT: JAI Press, pp. 235–249.

Benton, T. (1991) Biology and social science: why the return of the repressed should be given a (cautious) welcome. *Sociology*, 25, 1, 1–29.

Benveniste, J., LeCouteur, A. and Hepworth, J. (1999) Lay theories of anorexia nervosa: a discourse. *Journal of Health Psychology*, 4, 1: 59–69.

Berger, P. and Luckman, T. (1967) *The Social Construction of Reality: A Treatise in the Sociology of Knowledge*. New York: Doubleday.

Berkman, L.F. and Syme, S.L. (1979) Social networks, host resistance and mortality: a nine year follow up study of Alameda County residents. *American Journal of Epidemiology*, 109, 186–204.

Billig, M., Condor, S., Edwards, D., Gane, M., Middleton, D. and Radley, A. (1988) *Ideological Dilemmas: A Social Psychology of Everyday Thinking*. London: Sage.

Blalock, H.M. (1982) *Conceptualisation and Measurement in the Social Sciences*. London: Sage.

Bloch, I. (1909) *The Sexual Life of Our Time, in its Relations to Modern Civilisation*, trans. from the 6th German edn by M. Eden Paul. London: Rebman.

Bloor, D. (1976) *Knowledge and Social Imagery*. London: Routledge & Kegan Paul.

Bloor, M. and McIntosh, J. (1990) 'Surveillance and concealment: a comparison of techniques of client resistance in therapeutics communities and health visiting'. In S. Cunningham-Burley and N. McKeganey (eds), *Readings in Medical Sociology*. London: Routledge.

Brenner, M.H. (1977) Health costs and benefits of economic policy. *International Journal of Health Services*, 7, 581–623.

Brown, G.W. and Harris, T.O. (1978) *Social Origins of Depression*. New York: Free Press.

Brown, G.W. and Harris, T.O. (eds) (1989) *Life Events and Illness*. New York: Guilford Press.

Brown, R. (1986) *Social Psychology: The Second Edition*. New York: Free Press.

Brubaker, C. and Wickersham, D. (1990) Encouraging the practice of testicular self examination: a field application of the theory of reasoned action. *Health Psychology*, 9, 154–163.

Bruch, H. (1974) *Eating Disorders: Anorexia, Obesity and the Person Within*. London and Boston: Routledge & Kegan Paul.

Bruch, H. (1985) Four decades of eating disorders. In D.M. Garner and P.E. Garfinkel (eds), *Handbook of Psychotherapy for Anorexia Nervosa and Bulimia*. New York: Guilford Press.

Bruner, J. (1986) *Actual Minds, Possible Worlds*. Cambridge, MA: Harvard University Press.

Bruner, J. (1990) *Acts of Meaning*. Cambridge, MA: Harvard University Press.

Bryman, A. (1988) *Quantity and Quality in Social Research*. London: Routledge.

Burman, E. and Parker, I. (1993). Introduction – discourse analysis: the turn to the text. In E. Burman and I. Parker (eds), *Discourse Analytic Research*. London: Routledge.

Bush, J.W. (1983) *Quality of Well Being Scale: Function Status Profile and Symptom/ Problem Complex Questionnaire*. University of California, San Diego: Health Policy Project.

Calnan, M. (1987) *Health & Illness: The Lay Perspective*. London: Tavistock.

Cannon, W.B. (1932) *The Wisdom of the Body*. New York: Norton.

Carroll, D., Bennett, P. and Davey Smith, G. (1993) Socio-economic health inequalities: their origins and implications. *Psychology and Health*, 8, 295–316.

Carroll, D., Davey Smith, G. and Bennett, P. (1996) Some observations on health and socio-economic status. *Journal of Health Psychology*, 1, 1, 23–39.

Charles C., Redko C., Whelan, T., Gafni, A. and Reyno, L. (1998) Doing nothing is no choice: lay constructions of treatment decision-making among women with early-stage breast cancer. *Sociology of Health & Illness*, 20, 1, 71–95.

Charles, N. and Walters, V. (1998) Age and gender in women's accounts of their health: interviews with women in South Wales. *Sociology of Health & Illness*, 20, 3, 331–350.

Chase, S.E. (1995) *Interpreting Experience: The Narrative Study of Lives*. London: Sage.

Chernin, K. (1981) *The Obsession: Reflections on the Tyranny of Slenderness*. New York: Harper and Row.

Cooper, P.J. and Fairburn, C.G. (1986) The depressive symptoms of Bulimia Nervosa. *British Journal of Psychiatry*, 148, 268–274.

Cooper, P.T. and Taylor, M.J. (1988) Body image disturbance in Bulimia Nervosa. *British Journal of Psychiatry*, 153, 32–36.

Cooper, Z. and Fairburn, C.G. (1987) The Eating Disorder Examination: a semi structured interview for the assessment of the specific psychopathology of eating disorders. *International Journal of Eating Disorders*, 6, 1–8.

Creswell, J.W. (1998) *Qualitative Inquiry and Research Design*. London: Sage.

Crisp, A.H. (1984) The psychopathology of Anorexia Nervosa: getting the 'heat' out of the system. In A.J. Stunkard and E. Stellar (eds), *Eating and its Disorders*. New York: Raven Press, pp. 209–234.

Crossley, M. (1998) Sick role or empowerment: the ambiguities of life with an HIV positive diagnosis. *Sociology of Health and Illness*, 20, 507–531.

Crossley, M. (2000) *Rethinking Health Psychology*. Buckingham: Open University Press.

Csikszentmihalyi, M. (1992) *Flow: The Psychology of Happiness*. London: Rider Press.

Cushman, P. (1990) Why the self is empty: towards a historically situated psychology. *American Psychologist*, 45, 599–611.

Danziger, K. (1990) *Constructing the Subject*. Cambridge: Cambridge University Press.

Davey Smith, G. (1996) Income inequality and mortality: why are they related? *British Medical Journal*, 312, 987–988.

Davey Smith, G., Barley, M. and Blane, D. (1990) The Black Report on socio-economic inequalities in health 10 years on. *British Medical Journal*, 301, 373–377.

Davey Smith, G., Carroll, D., Rankin, S. and Rowan, D. (1992) Socioeconomic differentials in mortality: evidence from Glasgow graveyards. *British Medical Journal*, 305, 1554–1557.

Department of Health (1989) *Working for Patients*. London: HMSO.

Dey, I. (1993) *Qualitative Data Analysis*. London: Routledge.

Dickinson, A. (1980) *Contemporary Animal Learning Theory*. Cambridge: Cambridge University Press.

Dolce, J.J. (1987) Self efficacy and disability beliefs in the behavioural treatment of pain. *Behaviour Research and Therapy*, 25, 289.

Donaldson, M. (1992) *Human Minds: An Exploration*. Harmondsworth: Allen Lane.

Donovan, J. (1984) Ethnicity and health: a research review. *Social Science and Medicine*, 19, 663–670.

Douglas, M. (1966) *Purity and Danger: An Analysis of the Concepts of Pollution and Taboo*. London: Routledge & Kegan Paul.

Duden, B. (1991) *The Woman Beneath the Skin: A Doctor's Patients in Eighteenth-Century Germany*. London: Harvard University Press.

Durkheim, E. (1915) *The Elementary Forms of Religious Life: A Study of Religious Sociology*. London: Allen & Unwin.

Durkheim, E. (1938) *The Rules of Sociological Method*. New York: The Free Press.

Dzewaltowski, D.A. (1989) Toward a model of exercise motivation. *Journal of Sport and Exercise Psychology*, 11, 251–269.

Eiser, R. (1996) Reconnecting the individual and the social in health psychology. *Psychology and Health*, 11, 605–618.

Elias, N. (1978) *The Civilizing Process*. Oxford: Basil Blackwell. Originally published 1939.

Ellmann, L. (1988) *Sweet Desserts*. London: Penguin.

Engel, G.L. (1977) The need for a new medical model: a challenge for biomedicine. *Science*, 196, 129–135.

Engel, G.L. (1980) The clinical application of the biopsychosocial model. *American Journal of Psychiatry*, 137, 535–544.

Eyer, J. (1977) Does unemployment cause the death rate peak in each business cycle? A multifactorial model of death rate change. *International Journal of Health Services*, 7, 625–662.

Fairburn, C. (1984) Bulimia: its epidemiology and management. In A.J. Stunkard and E. Stellar (eds), *Eating and its Disorders*. New York: Raven Press.

Fallowfield, L. (1990) *The Quality of Life: The Missing Measurement in Health Care*. London: Souvenir Press.

Figlio, K. (1987) The lost subject of medical sociology. In Graham Scambler (ed.), *Sociological Theory and Medical Sociology*. London: Tavistock Publications, Chapter 4.

Fishbein, M. (1967) Attitude and the prediction of behaviour. In M. Fishbein (ed.), *Readings in Attitude Theory and Measurement*. New York: Wiley.

Fitzpatrick, R.M. (1982) Social concepts of disease and illness. In D.L. Patrick and G. Scambler (eds), *Sociology as Applied to Medicine*. London: Bailliere Tindall.

Flowers, P., Smith, J.A., Sheeran, P. and Beail, N. (1997) Health and romance: understanding unprotected sex in relationships between gay men. *British Journal of Health Psychology*, 2, 73–86.

Forel, A. (1906) *The Sexual Question: A Scientific Psychological Hygienic and Sociological Study*, trans. C.F. Marshall. Brooklyn, NY: Physicians and Surgeons Books.

Foucault, M. (1973) *The Birth of the Clinic: An Archeology of Medical Perception*. London: Tavistock.

Foucault, M. (1979a) *The History of Sexuality, Volume 1: An Introduction*. London: Allen Lane.

Foucault, M. (1979b) *Discipline and Punish: The Birth of the Prison*. London: Allen Lane.

Foucault, M. (1981) *The History of Sexuality, Volume 1*. Harmondsworth: Pelican.

Freeling, P. (1983) *A Workbook for Trainees in General Practice*. Bristol: Wright.

Freud, S. (1933) *2. New Introductory Lectures on Psychoanalysis*, trans. W.E.H. Sprott. First English translation: London and New York.

Garfinkel, H. (1967) *Studies in Ethnomethodology*. New York: Prentice Hall.

Garfinkel, H. (1984) *Studies of Ethnomethodology*. Cambridge: Polity Press.

Garfinkel, P.E. and Garner, D.M. (1986) *Anorexia Nervosa: A Multidimensional Perspective*. New York: Brunner/Mazel.

Garner, D.M. and Garfinkel, P.E. (1979) The Eating Attitudes Test: an index of the symptoms of anorexia nervosa. *Psychological Medicine*, 9, 272–279.

Garnham, A. (1985) *Psycholinguistics: Central Topics*. London: Methuen.

Gatchel, R.J., Baum, A. and Krantz, D.S. (1989) *An Introduction to Health Psychology*. New York: McGraw-Hill.

Gergen, K. (1973) Social psychology as history. *Journal of Personality and Social Psychology*, 26, 309–20.

Gergen, K. (1991) *The Saturated Self*. New York: Basic Books.

Giddens, A. (1991) *Modernity and Self Identity: Self and Society in the Later Modern Age*. Cambridge: Polity Press.

Gilchrist, L.D. and Schinke, S.P. (1983) Coping with contraception: cognitive and behavioural methods with adolescence. *Cognitive Therapy and Research*, 7, 379–388.

Gill, R. (1993) Justifying injustice: broadcasters' accounts of inequality in radio. In E. Burman and I. Parker (eds), *Discourse Analytic Research*. London: Routledge.

Glaser, B. and Strauss, A. (1967) *Awareness of Dying*. Chicago: Aldine.

Glynn, S.M. and Ruderman, A.J. (1986) The development and validation of an Eating Self Efficacy Scale. *Cognitive Therapy and Research*, 10, 403–420.

Goffman, E. (1961) *Asylums: Essays on the Social Situation of Mental Patients and Other Inmates*. Harmondsworth: Pelican Books.

Goldberg, D.P. (1978) *Manual of the General Health Questionnaire*. Windsor: NFER-Nelson.

Goldschneider, A. (1920) *Das Schmerz Problem*. Berlin: Springer.

Grant, M., Padilla, G.V., Ferrell, B.R. and Rhiner, M. (1990) Assessment of quality of life with a single instrument. *Seminars in Oncology Nursing*, 6, 260–270.

Harré, R. (1983) *Personal Being*. Oxford: Blackwell.

Harré, R. and Gillett, G. (1994) *The Discursive Mind*. London: Sage.

Hart, N. (1985) *The Sociology of Health and Medicine*. Lancashire: Causeway Press.

Haynes, S.G., Feinleib, M. and Kannel, W.B. (1980) The relationship of psycho-social factors to coronary heart disease in the Framingham study. III: Eight year incidence of coronary heart disease. *American Journal of Epidemiology*, 111, 37–58.

Heather, N. and Robertson, I. (1989) *Problem Drinking*. Oxford: Oxford University Press.

Heatherton, T.F. and Baumeister, R.F. (1991) Binge eating as an escape from self awareness. *Psychological Bulletin*, 110, 86–108.

Heider, F. (1958) *The Psychology of Interpersonal Relations*. New York: John Wiley.

Henriques, J., Hollway, W., Urwin, C., Venn, C. and Walkerdine, V. (1984) *Changing the Subject*. London: Methuen.

Herman, C.P. and Polivy J.A. (1984) A boundary model for the regulation of eating. In A.J. Stunkard and E. Stellar (eds), *Eating and its Disorders*. New York: Raven Press, pp. 141–156.

Herman, P. and Mack, D. (1975) Restrained and unrestrained eating. *Journal of Personality*, 43, 646–660.

Herman, C.P. and Polivy, J. (1975) Anxiety, restraint and eating behaviour. *Journal of Abnormal Psychology*, 84, 666–672.

Herman, C.P. and Polivy, J.A. (1989) Restraint and excess in dieters and bulimics. In K.M. Pirke and D. Ploog (eds), *The Psychobiology of Bulimia*. Heidelberg: Springer Verlag.

Hibscher, J.A. and Herman, C.P. (1977) Obesity, dieting, and the expression of 'obese' characteristics. *Journal of Comparative Physiological Psychology*, 91, 374–380.

Hill, D., Gardner, G. and Rassaby, J. (1985) Factors predisposing women to take precautions against breast and cervix cancer. *Journal of Applied Social Psychology*, 15, 1, 59–79.

Hite, S. (1976) *The Hite Report on Female Sexuality*. London: Pandora Press.

Hite, S. (1981) *The Hite Report on Male Sexuality*. London: Optima.

Hite, S. (1987) *The Hite Report on Women and Love*. Harmondsworth: Penguin.

Holland, J., Ramazanoglu, C. and Scott, S. (1990a) Managing risk and experiencing danger: Tensions between government AIDS health education policy and young women's sexuality. *Gender and Education*, 2, 125–146.

Holland, J., Ramazanoglu, C., Scott, S., Sharpe, S. and Thompson, R. (1990b) *Don't Die of Ignorance – I Nearly Died of Embarrassment: Condoms in Context*. London: Tufnell Press.

Humphrey, M. (1989) *Back Pain*. London: Routledge.

Hunt, S., McEwen, J. and McKenna, S.P. (1986) *Measuring Health Status*. London: Croom Helm.

Idler, E.L. and Kasl, S.V. (1995) Self ratings of health: Do they predict change in function as ability. *Journals of Gerontology Series B-Psychological Sciences and Social Sciences*, 50B, S344–S353.

James, V. and Gabe, J. (eds) (1996) *Health and the Sociology of Emotions*. Sociology of Health and Illness Monograph Series. Oxford: Blackwell.

Janz, N.K. and Becker, M.H. (1984) The health belief model: a decade later. *Health Education Quarterly*, 11, 1–47.

Jellinek, E.M. (1960) *The Disease Concept in Alcoholism*. New Brunswick, NJ: Hill House Press.

Jones, E.E. (1979) The rocky road from acts to dispositions. *American Psychologist*, 34, 107–117.

Kaplan, R.M. (1990) Behavior as the central outcome in health care. *American Psychologist*, 45, 1211–1220.

Kaplan, R.M., Sallis, J.F. and Patterson, T.L. (1993) *Health and Human Behaviour*. New York: McGraw-Hill.

Kaptein, A., Appels, A. and Orth Gormer, K. (eds) (2000) *Psychology in Medicine*. Houton, The Netherlands: Bohn Stafleu Van Loghum.

Katz, S., Downs, T.D., Cash, H.R. and Grotz, R.C. (1970) Progress in development of the index of ADL. *Gerontology*, 10, 20–30.

Kelleher, D. (1988) *Diabetes*. London: Routledge.

Kelly, G.A. (1955) The psychology of personal constructs. Vols 1 and 2, Norton: New York.

Kelly, G.A. (1980) The psychology of optimal man. In A.W. Landfield and L.M. Leitner (eds), *Personal Construct Psychology: Psychotherapy and Personality*. London: John Wiley.

Keys, A., Brozek, J., Henscel, A., Mickelson, O. and Taylor, H.L. (1950) *The Biology of Human Starvation*. Minneapolis, MN: University of Minnesota Press.

Kinsey, A.C., Pomeroy, W.B. and Martin, C.E. (1948) *Sexual Behaviour in the Human Male*. New York: W.B. Saunders.

Kinsey, A.C., Pomeroy, W.B., Martin, C.E. and Gebhard, P.H. (1953) *Sexual Behaviour in the Human Female*. New York: W.B. Saunders.

Kok, G., De Vries, H., Mudde, A.N. and Strecher, V.J. (1990) Planned health education and the role of self efficacy: Dutch research. *Health Education Research*, 5, 231–8.

Krantz, D.S., Glass, D.C., Contrada, R. and Miller, N.E. (1981) *Behavior and Health. National Science Foundation Second Five Year Outlook on Science and Technology*. Washington DC: US Government Printing Office.

Kuhn, T. (1962) *The Structure of Scientific Revolutions*. Chicago, IL: Chicago University Press.

Lalljee, M. (1996) The interpreting self: an experimentalist perspective. In R. Stevens (ed.), *Understanding the Self*. London: Sage.

Lasch, C. (1984) *The Minimal Self*. London: Pan Books.

Latour, B. (1987) *Science in Action*. Milton Keynes: Open University Press.

Latour, B. and Woolgar, S. (1986) *Laboratory Life: The Construction of Scientific Facts*, 2nd edn. Princeton, NJ: Princeton University Press.

Lawrence, L. (1984) *The Anorexic Experience*. London: The Women's Press Handbook Series.

Lawton, M.P., Moss, M. and Glicksman, A. (1990) The quality of life in the last year of life of older persons. *The Millbank Quarterly*, 68, 1–28.

Lazarfeld, P.F. (1958) Evidence and inference in social research. *Daedalus*, 87, 99–130.

Lazarus, R.S. (1975) A cognitively oriented psychologist looks at biofeedback. *American Psychologist*, 30, 553–561.

Lazarus, R.S. and Cohen, J.B. (1977) Environmental stress. In L. Altman and J.F. Wohlwill (eds), *Human Behavior and the Environment: Current Theory and Research*. New York: Plenum, Vol. 2, pp. 89–127.

Lazarus, R.S. and Folkman, S. (1987) Transactional theory and research on emotions and coping. *European Journal of Personality*, 1, 141–170.

Leventhal, H. and Nerenz, D. (1985) The assessment of illness cognition. In P. Karoly (ed.), *Measurement Strategies in Health Psychology*. New York: Wiley & Sons, pp. 517–554.

Lévi-Strauss, C. (1965) Le triangle culinaire. *L'Arc*, 26, 19–29.

Ley, P. (1988) *Communicating with Patients*. London: Croom Helm.

Litt, M.D. (1988) Self efficacy and perceived control: cognitive mediators of pain tolerance. *Journal of Personality and Social Psychology*, 54, 149–160.

Loro, A.D. and Orleans, C.S. (1981) Binge eating in obesity: preliminary findings and guidelines for behavioural analysis and treatment. *Addictive Behaviours*, 7, 155–166.

Loveday, L. and Chiba, S. (1985) Partaking with the divine and symbolizing the societal: the semiotics of Japanese food and drink. *Semiotics*, 56, 115–131.

Lynch, J.W. and Kaplan, G.A. (1997) Understanding how inequality in the distribution of income affects health. *Journal of Health Psychology*, 2, 3, 297–314.

Lynch, M. and Woolgar, S. (1988) Introduction: Sociological orientations to representational practice in science. In M. Lynch and S. Woolgar (eds), *Representation in Scientific Practice*. Amsterdam: Kluwer Academic.

McGee, H.M., O'Boyle, C.A., Hickey, A., O'Malley, K. and Joyce, C.R. (1991) Assessing the quality of life of the individual: the SEIQoL with a healthy and a gastroenterology unit population. *Psychological Medicine*, 21, 749–759.

Macintyre, S. (1986) The patterning of health by social position in contemporary Britain: directions for sociological research. *Social Science and Medicine*, 23, 4, 393–415.

McKeown, T. (1979) *The Role of Medicine*. Oxford: Blackwell.

Mackintosh, N.J. (1974) *The Psychology of Animal Learning*. London: Academic Press.

McNeil, B.J., Pauker, S.G., Sox, H.C. and Tversky, A. (1982) On the elicitation of preferences for alternative therapies. *New England Journal of Medicine*, 306, 1259–1262.

Manning, M.M. and Wright, T.L. (1983) Self efficacy expectancies, outcome expectancies and the persistence of pain control in child birth. *Journal of Personality and Social Psychology*, 45, 421–431.

Marks, D.F. (1996) Editorial. *Journal of Health Psychology*, 1, 1, 5–6.

Marks, D.F., Brucher-Albers, C., Donker, F.J.S., Jepsen, Z., Rodriguez-Marin, J., Sidot, S. and Backman, B.W. (1998) Health Psychology 2000: the development of professional health psychology. *Journal of Health Psychology*, 3, 1.

Marlatt, G.A. and Gordon, J.R. (1980) Determinants of relapse: implications for the maintenance of behaviour change. In P. Davidson (ed.), *Behavioural Medicine: Changing Health Lifestyles*. New York: Brunner & Mazel.

Marlatt, G.A. and Gordon, J.R. (1985) *Relapse Prevention*. New York: Guilford Press.

Marmot, M. (1999) Introduction. In M. Marmot and R.G. Wilkinson (eds), *Social Determinants of Health*. Oxford: Oxford University Press.

Marmot, M. and Brunner, E. (1999) Social organisation, stress and health. In M. Marmot and R.G. Wilkinson (eds), *Social Determinants of Health*. Oxford: Oxford University Press.

Marmot, M.G. and Theorell, T. (1988) Social class and cardiovascular disease: the contribution of work. *International Journal of Health Services*, 18, 659–674.

Marx, K. (1849) Wage labour and capital. In *Marx and Engels Selected Works*. London: Lawrence & Wishart (1968 edn).

Masters, W. and Johnson, V. (1966) *Human Sexual Response*. Boston, MA: Little Brown.

Masters, W. and Johnson, V. (1970) *Human Sexual Inadequacy*. Boston, MA: Little Brown.

Meenan, R.F., Gertman, P.M. and Mason, J.H. (1980) Measuring health status in arthritis: the arthritis impact measurement scales. *Arthritis and Rheumatism*, 23, 146–152.

Melzack, R. (1975) The McGill pain questionnaire: major properties and scoring methods. *Pain*, 1, 277–299.

Melzack, R. (1979) *The Puzzle of Pain*. New York: Basic Books.

Melzack, R. and Wall, P.D. (1965) Pain mechanisms: a new theory. *Science*, 150, 971–979.

Melzack, R. and Wall, P.D. (1982) *The Challenge of Pain*. New York: Basic Books.

Mennell, S. (1985) *All Manners of Food: Eating and Taste in England and France from the Middle Ages to the Present*. Oxford: Basil Blackwell.

Mennell, S. (1986) *Prospects for the History of Food*. Groniek: Gronings Historisch Tijdschrift, 95, 7–21.

Mennell, S., Murcott, A. and Van Otterloo, A.H. (1992) *The Sociology of Food: Eating Diet and Culture*. London: Sage.

Milgram, S. (1961) Nationality and conformity. *Scientific American*, 205, December, 45–51.

Milgram, S. (1974) *Obedience to Authority*. New York: Harper & Row; London: Tavistock.

Moos, R.H. and Schaefer, J.A. (1984) The crisis of physical illness: an overview and conceptual approach. In R.H. Moos (ed.), *Coping with Physical Illness: New Perspectives*, New York: Plenum, Vol. 2, pp. 3–25.

Morgan, M., Calnan, M. and Manning, N. (1985) *Sociological Approaches to Health and Medicine*. London: Routledge.

Morse, J.M. (1994) *Critical Issues in Qualitative Research Methods*. London: Sage.

Moscovici, S. (1972) Society and theory in social psychology. In J. Israel and H. Tajfel (eds), *The Context of Social Psychology: A Critical Assessment*. London: Academic Press.

Mulkay, M. (1991) *Sociology of Science: A Sociological Pilgrimage*. Milton Keynes: Open University Press.

Murcott, A. (1983) *The Sociology of Food and Eating*. Aldershot: Gower.

Murray, M. and Chamberlain, K. (eds) (1999) *Qualitative Health Psychology: Theories and Methods*. London: Sage.

Nathanson, C.A. (1977) Sex, illness and medical care: a review of data, theory and method. *Social Science and Medicine*, 11, 13–25.

Nettleton, S. (1995) *The Sociology of Health and Illness*. Cambridge: Polity Press.

Nisbett R.E. (1972) Hunger, obesity and the ventromedial hypothalamus. *Psychological Review*, 79, 433–453.

Norman, P. and Smith, L. (1995) The theory of planned behaviour and exercise: an investigation into the role of prior behaviour, behavioural intentions and attitude variability. *European Journal of Social Psychology*, 25, 403–415.

North, D., Davis, P. and Powell, A. (1995) Patient responses to benzodiazepine medication: a typology of adaptive repertoires developed by long-term users. *Sociology of Health & Illness*, 17, 5, 632–650.

O'Boyle, C.A., McGee, H., Hickey, A., O'Malley, K. and Joyce, C.R. (1992) Individual quality of life in patients undergoing hip replacement. *Lancet*, 339, 1088–1091.

Ogden, J. (1992) *Fat Chance! The Myth of Dieting Explained.* London and New York: Routledge.

Ogden, J. (1994) The effects of smoking cessation, restrained eating, and motivational states on food intake in the laboratory. *Health Psychology*, 13, 114–121.

Ogden, J. (1995a) Psychosocial theory and the creation of the risky self. *Social Science and Medicine*, 40, 409–415.

Ogden, J. (1995b) Changing the subject of health psychology. *Psychology and Health*, 10, 257–265.

Ogden, J. (2000) *Health Psychology: A Textbook* (2nd edn). Buckingham: Open University Press.

Ogden, J. and Greville, L. (1993) Cognitive changes to preloading in restrained and unrestrained eaters as measured by the Stroop task. *International Journal of Eating Disorders*, 14, 185–196.

Ogden, J. and Wardle, J. (1991) Cognitive and Emotional Responses to Food. *International Journal of Eating Disorders*, 10, 297–311.

Parsons, T. (1951) *The Social System.* London: Routledge.

Patrick, D.L. and Ericson, P.E (1993) *Health Status and Health Policy: Allocating Resources to Health Care.* Oxford: Oxford University Press.

Pavlov, I.P. (1927) *Conditioned Reflexes.* Oxford: Oxford University Press.

Pearce, J.M. and Hall, H. (1980) A model for Pavlovian learning: variations in the effectiveness of conditioned but not of unconditioned stimuli. *Psychological Review*, 87, 532–539.

Piaget, J. (1954) *The Construction of Reality in the Child.* New York: Basic Books.

Piette, A. (1989) Folklore ou esthetique du brouillage. *Recherches sociologiques*, 20, 177–190.

Pill, R. and Stott, N.C.H. (1982) Concepts of illness causation and responsibility: some preliminary data from a sample of working class mothers. *Social Science and Medicine*, 16, 315–322.

Popper, K.R. (1959) *The Logic of Scientific Discovery.* New York: Basic Books.

Porter, R. and Hall, L. (1995) *The Facts of Life: The Creation of Sexual Knowledge in Britain, 1650–1950.* New Haven, CT, and London: Yale University Press.

Potter, J. and Edwards, D. (1992) *Discursive Psychology.* London: Sage.

Potter, J. and Wetherell, M. (1987) *Discourse and Social Psychology: Beyond Attitudes and Behaviour.* London: Sage.

Pound, P., Gompertz, P. and Ebrahim, S. (1998) Illness in the context of older age: the case of stroke. *Sociology of Health & Illness*, 20, 4, 489–506.

Premack, D. and Woodruff, G. (1978) Does the chimpanzee have a theory of mind? *The Behavioural and Brain Sciences*, 1, 515–526.

Radley, A. (1993) The role of metaphor in adjustment to chronic illness. In *Worlds of Illness: Biographical and Cultural Perspectives on Health and Disease.* London: Routledge, Chapter 6.

Radley. A. (1994) *Making Sense of Illness.* London: Sage.

Radley, A. (1997) What role does the body have in illness? In L. Yardley (ed.), *Material Discourses of Health and Illness.* London: Routledge.

Rainwater, J. (1989) *Self Therapy.* London: Crucible.

Reid, I. (1989) *Social Class Differences in Britain*, 3rd edn. London: Fontana.

Rescorla, R.A. (1967) Pavlovian conditioning and its proper control procedures. *Psychological Review*, 74, 71–80.

Rescorla, R.A. and Wagner, A.R. (1972) A theory of Pavlovian conditioning:

variations in the effectiveness of reinforcement and non-reinforcement. In A.H. Black and W.F. Prokasy (eds), *Classical Conditioning Vol. 11: Current Research and Theory*. New York: Appleton-Century-Crofts, pp. 64–99.

Richards, A. (1932) *Hunger and Work in a Savage Tribe. A Functional Study of Nutrition Among the Southern Bantu*. London: Routledge.

Robinson, I. (1988) *Multiple Sclerosis*. London: Routledge.

Rogers, R.W. (1983) Cognitive and physiological processes in fear appeals and attitude change: a revised theory of protection motivation. In J.R. Cacioppo and R.E. Petty (eds), *Social Psychology: A Source Book*. New York: Guilford, pp. 153–176.

Rosaldo, M. (1984) Toward an anthropology of self and feeling. In R.A. Schweder and R.A. LeVine (eds), *Culture Theory: Essays on Mind, Self, and Emotion*. Cambridge: CUP.

Rose, N. (1985) *The Psychological Complex*. London: Routledge.

Rose, N. (1990) *Governing the Soul*. London: Routledge.

Rosenhan, D.L. (1973) On being sane in insane place. *Science*, 179, 250–258.

Rosenstock, I.M. (1966) Why people use health services. *Millbank Memorial Fund Quarterly*, 44, 94.

Rosenstock, I.M., Strecher, V.J. and Becker, M.H. (1988) Social learning theory and the Health Belief Model. *Health Education Quarterly*, 15, 175–183.

Rosser, R.M. and Kind, P. (1978) A scale of valuations of states of illness: is there a social consensus? *International Journal of Epidemiology*, 7, 347–358.

Rowntree, B. Seebohm (1901) *Poverty: A Study of Town Life*. London: Macmillan.

Russell, G.F.M. (1979) Bulimia nervosa: an ominous variant of anorexia nervosa. *Psychological Medicine*, 9, 429–448.

Sarafino, E.P. (1990) *Health Psychology: Biopsychosocial Interactions*. New York: John Wiley.

Schachter, S. (1968). Obesity and eating. *Science*, 161, 751–756.

Schachter, S. and Gross, L. (1968) Manipulated time and eating behaviour. *Journal of Personality and Social Psychology*, 10, 98–106.

Schachter, S. and Rodin, J. (1974) *Obese Humans and Rats*. Potomac, MD: Erlbaum.

Schachter, S., Goldman, R. and Gordon, A. (1968) Effects of fear, food deprivation and obesity on eating. *Journal of Personality and Social Psychology*, 10, 91–97.

Schou, K.C. and Hewison, J. (1998) Health psychology and discourse: personal accounts as social texts in grounded theory. *Journal of Health Psychology*, 3, 3, 297–312.

Schwarzer, R. (1992) Self efficacy in the adoption and maintenance of health behaviours: theoretical approaches and a new model. In R. Schwarzer (ed.), *Self Efficacy: Thought Control of Action*. Washington, DC: Hemisphere.

Segal, L. (1994) *Straight Sex: The Politics of Pleasure*. London: Virago.

Seligman, M.E.P. (1975) *Helplessness: On Depression, Development and Death*. San Francisco, CA: W.H. Freeman.

Seydal, E., Taal, E. and Weigman, O. (1990) Risk appraisal, outcome and self efficacy expectancies: cognitive factors in preventative behaviour related to cancer. *Psychology and Health*, 4, 99–109.

Seyle, H. (1956) *The Stress of Life*. New York: McGraw-Hill.

Sheridan, C.L. and Radmacher, S.A. (1992) *Health Psychology: Challenging the Biomedical Model*. New York: Wiley.

Shisslak, C.M., Paxda, S.L. and Crago, M. (1990) Body weight and bulimia as discriminators of psychological characteristics among anorexic, bulimic and obese women. *Journal of Abnormal Psychology*, 99, 380–384.

Shute, J. (1992) *Life-Size*. London: Mandarin Paperbacks.

Silverman, D. (1993) *Interpreting Qualitative Data*. London: Sage.

Silverman, D. (2000) *Doing Qualitative Research*. London: Sage.

Skinner, B.F. (1953) *Science and Human Behavior*. New York: Macmillan.

Smith, J.A. (1996) Beyond the divide between cognition and discourse: using interpretative phenomenological analysis in health psychology. *Psychology and Health*, 11, 261–271.

Smith, J., Hare, R. and Van Lagenhove, L. (eds) (1995) *Rethinking Methods in Psychology*. London: Sage.

Smith, M.B. (1994) Selfhood at risk: postmodern perils and the perils of postmodernism. *American Psychologist*, May, 405–411.

Sontag, S. (1977) *Illness as Metaphor*. London: Allen Lane, Penguin Books.

Spencer, J.A. and Fremouw, M.J. (1979) Binge eating as a function of restraint and weight classification. *Journal of Abnormal Psychology*, 88, 262–267.

Spitzer, L. and Rodin, J. (1981) Human eating behaviour: a critical review of studies in normal weight and overweight individuals. *Appetite*, 2, 293–329.

Stacey, M. (1988) *The Sociology of Health and Healing. A Textbook*. London: Unwin Hyman.

Stainton Rogers, W. (1991) *Explaining Health and Illness: An Exploration of Diversity*. London: Harvester Wheatsheaf.

Stevens, R. (ed.) (1996a) *Understanding the Self*. London: Sage.

Stevens, R. (1996b) Introduction: Making sense of the person in a social world. In R. Stevens (ed.), *Understanding the Self*. London: Sage.

Stevens, R. (1996c) The reflexive self: an experiential perspective. In R. Stevens (ed.), *Understanding the Self*. London: Sage.

Stewart, A.L. and Ware, J.E. (eds) (1992) *Measuring Functioning and Well Being: The Medical Outcomes Study Approach*. Durham, NC: Duke University Press.

Stopes, M. (1926) *Sex and the Young*. London: Gill.

Sutherland, N.S. (1973) Object recognition. In E.D. Carterette and M.P. Friedman (eds), *Handbook of Perception. Volume 3: Biology of Perceptual Systems*. London: Academic Press, pp. 157–206.

Szasz, T.S. (1961) *The Myth of Mental Illness*. New York: Harper & Row.

Tajfel, H. and Fraser, C. (eds) (1978) *Introducing Social Psychology: An Analysis of Individual Reaction and Response*. London: Penguin.

Taylor, C.B., Bandura, A., Ewart, C.K., Miller, N.H. and DeBusk, R.F. (1985) Exercise testing to enhance wives' confidence in the husbands' cardiac capability soon after clinically uncomplicated acute myocardial infarction. *American Journal of Cardiology*, 55, 635–638.

Taylor, S.E. (1983) Adjustment to threatening events: A theory of cognitive adaptation. *American Psychologist*, 38, 1161–1173.

Thomas, K. (1996) The defensive self: a psychodynamic perspective. In R. Stevens (ed.), *Understanding the Self*. London: Sage.

Thompson, R. and Scott, S. (1990) *Learning about sex: young women and the social construction of sexual identity*. WRAP paper 4. London: The Tufnell Press.

Toates, F. (1996) The embodied self: a biological perspective. In R. Stevens (ed.), *Understanding the Self*. London: Sage.

Turner, B. (1982) The discourse of diet. *Theory, Culture and Society*, 1, 23–32.

Turner, B. (1992) *Regulating Bodies*. London: Routledge.

Van Otterloo, A.H. (1990) *Eten en eetlust in Nederland 1940–1990. Een historisch-socioligische studie*. Amsterdam: Bert Bakker.

Vanneman, R. and Cannon, W. (1987) *The American Perception of Class*. Philadelphia, PA: Temple University Press.

Vanneman, R. and Pampel, F.C. (1977) The American perception of class and status. *American Sociological Review*, 42, 422–437.

Von Frey, M. (1895) *Untersuchungen Über die Sinnesfunctionen der Menschlichen Haut Erste Abhandlung: Druckempfindung und Schmerz*. Leipzig: Hirzel.

Von Krafft-Ebing, R. (1894) *Psychopathia Sexualis with Especial Reference to Contrary Sexual Instinct: A Medical Legal Study*, 7th enlarged, revised edn, trans. Charles Gilbert Chaddock. Philadelphia: Davis.

Wagner, A.R. (1969) Stimulus selection and a 'modified continuity theory'. In G.H. Bower and J.T. Spence (eds), *The Psychology of Learning and Motivation*. New York: Academic Press, Vol. 3, pp. 1–43.

Wagner, S., Halmi, K.A. and Maguire, T. (1987) The sense of personal ineffectiveness in patients with eating disorders. *International Journal of Eating Disorders*, 6, 495–505.

Wallston, K.A. and Wallston, B.S. (1982) Who is responsible for your health? The construct of health locus of control. In G.S. Sanders and J. Suls (eds), *Social Psychology of Health and Illness*. Hillsdale, NJ: Erlbaum, pp. 65–95.

Ware, J.E. and Sherbourne, C.D. (1992) The MOS 36 item short form health survey (SF-36). Conceptual framework and item selection. *Medical Care*, 30, 473–483.

Ware, J.E., Brook, R.H. and Rogers, W.H. (1986) Comparison of health outcomes at a health maintenance organisation with those of fee for service care. *Lancet*, 1, 1017–1022.

Watson, J.D. (1968) *The Double Helix: A Personal Account of the Discovery of the Structure of DNA*. Harmondsworth: Penguin.

Weeks, J. (1985) *Sexuality and its Discontents: Meanings, Myths and Sexualities*. London: Routledge & Kegan Paul.

Weinman, J. (1982) *An Outline of Psychology as Applied to Medicine*. Bristol: Wright.

Weisenberg, M. (1977) Pain and pain control. *Psychological Bulletin*, 84, 1004–1008.

Wellings, K., Field, J., Johnson, A.M. and Wadsworth, J. (1994) *Sexual Behaviour in Britain: The National Survey of Sexual Attitudes and Lifestyles*. London: Penguin.

Wetherell, M. and Maybin, J. (1996) The distributed self: a social constructionist perspective. In R. Stevens (ed.), *Understanding the Self*. London: Sage.

Wetherell, M. and Potter, J. (1992) *Mapping the Language of Racism: Discourse and the Legitimation of Exploitation*. Hassocks, Sussex: Harvester/Wheatsheaf.

Whitehead, M. (1995) Tackling inequalities: a review of policy initiatives. In M. Benzeval, K. Judge and M. Whitehead (eds), *Tackling Inequalities in Health: An Agenda for Action*. London: King's Fund, pp. 22–52.

WHO (1981) *Global Strategy for Health for All by the Year 2000*. Geneva: World Health Organisation.

WHOQOL Group (1993) *Measuring Quality of Life: The Development of a World Health Organisation Quality of Life instrument (WHOQOL)*. Geneva: WHO.

Wiedenfeld, S.A., O'Leary, A., Bandura, A., Brown, S., Levine, S. and Raska, K.

(1990) Impact of perceived self efficacy in coping with stressors on immune function. *Journal of Personality and Social Psychology*, 59, 1082–1094.

Wiles, R. and Higgins, J. (1996) Doctor–patient relationships in the private sector: patients' perspectives. *Sociology of Health and Illness*, 18, 3, 341–356.

Wilkinson, R.G. (1989) Class mortality differentials, income distribution and trends in poverty 1921–81. *Journal of Social Policy*, 18, 307–335.

Wilkinson, R.G. (1990) Income distribution and mortality: a natural experiment. *Sociology of Health and Illness*, 12, 391–412.

Wilkinson, R.G. (1992) Income distribution and life expectancy. *British Medical Journal*, 304, 165–168.

Williams, D.R. and Collins, C. (1995) Socioeconomic and racial differences in health. *Annual Review of Sociology*, 21, 349–386.

Williams, G.J., Cahmove, A. and Millar, H.R. (1990) Eating disorders, perceived control, assertiveness and hostility. *British Journal of Clinical Psychology*, 29, 327–335.

Williams, S.J. and Bendelow, G. (1996) Emotions, health and illness: the 'missing link' in medical sociology? Chapter 1 in *Health and the Sociology of Emotions*, Sociology of Health and Illness Monograph Series. Oxford: Blackwell.

Willig, C. (1995) 'I wouldn't have married the guy if I'd have to do that': heterosexual adults' constructions of condom use and their implications for sexual practice. *Journal of Community and Applied Social Psychology*, 5, 75–87.

Winett, R.A. (1985) Eco-behavioural assessment in lifestyles: concepts and methods. In P. Karoly (ed.), *Measurement Strategies in Health Psychology*. New York: John Wiley.

Winnicott, D.W. (1960) Ego distortion in terms of true and false self. In D.W. Winnicott (ed.), *The Maturational Processes and the Facilitating Environment*. London: Hogarth Press.

Wallerstein, J. and Blakeslee, S. (1989) *Second Chances*. London: Bantam.

Woolgar, S. (1981) Interests and explanations in the study of social science. *Social Studies of Science*, 11, 365–397.

Woolgar, S. (1988) *Science: The Very Idea*. London: Ellis Horwood Ltd, Chichester and Tavistock Publications.

Yardley, L. (1997) Introducing material-discursive approaches to health and illness. In L. Yardley (ed.), *Material Discourses of Health and Illness*. London: Routledge, pp. 1–24.

Yardley, L. and Beech, S. (1998) 'I'm not a doctor': deconstructing accounts of coping, causes and control of dizziness. *Journal of Health Psychology*, 3, 3, 313–328.

Young, R. (1977) Science is social relations. *Radical Science Journal*, 5, 65–131.

Index

Index compiled by Frank Pert